trench fighting 1914-18

trench fighting 1914–18

Charles Messenger

BB

Editor-in-Chief: Barrie Pitt
Editor: David Mason
Art Director: Sarah Kingham
Picture Editor: Robert Hunt
Consultant Art Editor: Denis Piper
Designer: David A Evans
Illustration: John Batchelor
Photographic Research: Jonathan Moore
Cartographer: Richard Natkiel

First Printing: January 1972
Printed in United States of America

Ballantine Books Inc.
101 Fifth Avenue New York NY 10003

An Intext Publisher

Contents

The Techniques of survival

Introduction by John Keegan

The physical conditions of the fighting in the. First World War arouse both fascination and disbelief. How was it that the individual soldier put up with the cold, the wet, the dirt, the noise, the frequent death of comrades, the constant danger and the apparent inevitability, sooner or later, of personal extinction, perhaps cleanly by a bullet in the open but much more probably by multiple woundings by a shell, by suffocation in a trench cave-in or by shock and loss of blood before medical care could reach him? And how was it that the extraordinary trench environment in which the millions suffered this agony, came into being in the first place?

The second question is the rather easier to answer. It did not come about intentionally. Indeed, trench, siege, static or position warfare, as it might variously have been called before 1914, was anathema to the European armies of the period. All subscribed, with greater or lesser fervency, to a doctrine of war which laid its emphasis upon mobility and manoeuvre and upon the pursuit of swift decisions. Tactical training reflected this emphasis. Infantry was chiefly exercised in fire and movement, and artillery in the direct support role – that is to say in shooting at human targets at close range rather than at terrain features over long ranges. Neither of these two arms, any more than their still very numerous cavalry comrades had been instructed in the tedious, immobile, hole-in-corner business of trench warfare, and none of them was psychologically prepared or physically equipped to wage it. Unfortunately, their very efficiency in one of the techniques of 'open warfare' – the ability to put down vast volumes of fire for comparatively extended periods – meant that their freedom to practice the other, – rapid movement about the battlefield – was quite nullified. It took no more than a month of fighting for this point to make itself felt on the battlefields of the west, at the end

of which period a considerable length of what would soon be known as the Western Front had been entrenched. Attempts to win a decision on the 'open flank' of this trench system all failed, each failure leading to an extension of the trenches until the sea was reached.

The emergence of a continuosly entrenched front meant abandoning the hope of quick victory which had animated both sides at the outbreak. It did not mean however that any of the combatants slackened in their efforts to win the war. On the contrary those efforts, after a short interlude of exhaustion during the winter of 1914, were redoubled, which in terms of trench warfare entailed an enormous increase in the weight of artillery deployed behind the front and in the density of men committed to any attack. These were the only means of which the generals could think to break through the defences opposite their own.

This intensification of combat was mutual and progressive, and seemingly obeyed mathematical rather than human laws. Hence the inhumanity of its conditions and the helplessness which the individual subjected to those laws so very often felt. 'Attrition' 'materialschlacht', 'guerre de usure'; in whatever language soldiers sought to describe the character of trench warfare, they expressed the same idea.

It is a testimony to human adaptability that the soldiers of the First World War should nevertheless have contrived methods both to survive and to continue the fight in the trenches, and it is in this human defiance of inexorable circumstances which Charles Messenger has long been interested. His knowledge of the battalion and company level literature of the Western Front is almost unrivalled and he has drawn on it in this book to write one of the most perceptive narratives of 'France and Flanders 14-18' that is likely to appear for many a year,

Genesis

To most people, nowadays, the First World War is synonymous with trench fighting. In every theatre of the war the attacker was, at some time or other, faced with the problem of an attack on an entrenched enemy. Nowhere was this more apparent than on the Western Front, where for four years both sides were permanently involved in finding a satisfactory solution to this phenomenon. The techniques of trench fighting originated, for the most part, on the Western Front; if they were used elsewhere to start with it was only in order to prove them for use on the Western Front.

Trench warfare came about as a natural progression in the science of war. It was the American Civil War which first showed what lay ahead. Before this time trench warfare had been known, but only as a means of laying siege to a town, as in all 18th Century European wars, or as a technique of allowing one to draw breath after a hard campaign, such as Wellington's use of the lines of Torres Vedras during the winter of 1810-11. The wars of the 18th and first half of the 19th Centuries were fought with the musket, which was effective only up to a range of a hundred yards. The two key weapons on the battlefield were the cannon and the bayonet, and victory depended on the intelligent use of these more than anything else.

The development of the Minié rifle and the self-sealing cartridge, which gave the bullet greater propulsion and hence greater range, radically altered tactics on the battlefield. It soon became apparent in the American Civil War that the traditional frontal attack could no longer work. The increased range of the rifle meant that it was possible effectively to engage the attackers at a much greater range and consequently inflict heavier casualties on them. At the same time cannon became rifled, thereby increasing their range as well, and this all combined to produce the realisation that, even more than before, it was easier to defend than to attack. Defence was still easier, too, if one dug protective trenches in order to prevent casualties from the enemy's fire. Colonel Theodore Lyman, an officer on General Meade's Staff, wrote: 'Put a man in a hole and a good battery on a hill behind him, and he will beat off three times his number, even if he is not a very good soldier.' This, combined with the introduction of machine guns, Requa's and the Gatling, and the Spencer magazine breech-loading rifle, as well as the use of aerial observation in the shape of balloons, armoured trains, lamp and flag signalling and field telegraph, made the American Civil War the first of the modern wars.

In Europe it was the Prussians who paved the way with their shattering defeat in 1866 of the Austrian armies, held to be among the best in Europe at that time, in seven weeks. The reasons for this were firstly the inferiority of the Austrian General Staff, and, secondly, the advantages of the breech-loading as opposed to the muzzle-loading rifle. Although the Austrian Lorenz rifle had over twice the range of the Prussian needle-gun, the advantage of the latter was that it could be loaded lying down. This led General von Moltke, the Prussian Chief of Staff, to deduce: 'It is absolutely beyond all doubt that the man who shoots without stirring has the advantage of him who fires while advancing, that the one finds protection in the ground, whereas in it the other finds obstacles, and that, if to the most spirited dash one opposes a quiet steadiness, it is fire effect, nowadays so powerful, which will determine the issue.' He also realised that the day of the frontal attack was gone and that one '. . . must therefore turn towards the flanks of the enemy's position'.

Against the French in 1870 the

An early example of trench fighting: Confederate dead at Fredericksburg, May 1863

Helmuth von Moltke, architect of the Prussian victories over Austria and France in 1866 and 1870. He realised that with the advent of the muzzle-loading rifle the day of the frontal assault was gone

Prussians scored another resounding victory. The French had as ineffectual a General Staff as the Austrians, but had a superior breech-loading rifle, the Chassepot. However the Prussian breech-loading artillery was more than a match for the French muzzle-loading cannon. The French did have the mitrailleuse, a machine gun of twenty-five barrels sighted at 1,200 metres, but unfortunately, in order to maintain secrecy, it was not issued until just before hostilities began and, instead of being used by the infantry, was used as an artillery weapon, which meant that it was employed only at its extreme range. Whereas the French idea was to make maximum use of the superior range of the Chassepot by engaging the enemy at extreme range, then dig in and destroy him as he came up, the Prussians had different ideas. The theme of their doctrine was fire at all times. They would contain the French front and then get round to the flanks, all the

time covered by fire. Much of the time they were able to hold the French back by using concentrated artillery fire, which outranged the Chassepot. This was particularly successful at Sedan. It was also noticeable that there was only one successful cavalry charge during the whole war, that of Bredow's Brigade at Vionville. The horse was too vulnerable against modern firepower when used in the attack. Cavalry, however, were still important, especially for reconnaissance.

The years that followed the Franco-Prussian War were used by the French military thinkers to analyse the causes of their defeat and to produce a new doctrine. Above all else it was the aggressive energy of the Prussians that impressed them most. They therefore deduced that attack was the only means of forcing a favourable decision. In 1880 a book entitled *Etudes sur le Combat* was published. It had been compiled from notes found among the papers of a Colonel Ardant du Picq, who had been mortally wounded during the first month of the war with Prussia. He believed that morale was the most important single factor in war and that to achieve an ascendancy of morale over the enemy it was necessary to advance against him. 'Moral effect inspires fear. Fear must be changed into terror in order to conquer... The moral impulse lies in the perception by the enemy of the resolution which animates you. . . Manoeuvres are threats. He who appears the most threatening wins.' This was supported by Colonel Cardot, who occupied the influential position of chief of the *Ecole de Guerre* and as a result the official frontage of a division in attack was reduced from 2,800 to 1,600 metres in 1887. 'Brave and energetically commanded infantry can march under the most violent fire even against well-defended trenches, and take them.' Colonel Foch, who was to rise to the post of Generalissimo of the Allied forces in 1918, succeeded Cardot and preached the

Ferdinand Foch, advocate of the spirit of the offensive which was to cost France dearly after 1914

same gospel. In his *Des Principes de la Guerre* he succeeded in convincing himself mathematically that, provided one had numerical superiority, the attack must succeed over the defence. Unfortunately his calculations did not take into consideration the decreased effect of the attackers' fire on entrenched defenders. He did, however, appreciate the importance of gaining superiority of fire and realised the role of artillery in preparing the attack, rather than merely supporting it.

In a word the basis of the French theory of attack lay in the word *élan* , a quality which they believed that the French soldier alone possessed. Yet there were those who disagreed, like the brilliant military writer and critic Captain Mayer, who vehemently attacked Foch, envisaging instead a siege war which would last for years. The unbelievers. however, had little influence and merely put paid to any chances of promotion that they might have had. As a result of the theory the French army was trained to advance in the traditional Napoleonic style and to worship the power of the bayonet ('Rosalie'). In order to win the fire fight the French put all their efforts into producing the maximum amount of effective field artillery, in this case the famous '75'. The Germans also appreciated the increasing importance of artillery, but a study of the Russo-Japanese War convinced them that it was medium and heavy artillery, which would provide the answer to the riddle of the fire fight.

They also introduced centralised control of artillery fire at divisional and brigade level with a view to producing a joint infantry/artillery plan, unlike the French who treated the two as completely separate entities. Even greater emphasis was placed on fire combined with movement. 'The enemy will be held in front by fire and attacked in the flank: for every tactical group from the company upwards which attacks by fire, or manoeuvres under cover of fire, another will hold the enemy by fire and thus support the attacking group', as the German Infantry Manual of 1875 laid down. The introduction of the Mauser magazine rifle did away with the need for volley firing and infantry were also issued with entrenching tools.

The British army, which had not been involved in a major European War since 1815, took longer to adjust. The British went to war against the Boers in South Africa in 1899 convinced that their 'parade ground' tactics, which had been so successful against undisciplined and naive native opponents, were wholly sufficient to defeat a handful of unruly farmers. The flexibility and cunning of the Boer, armed with modern weapons supplied by Germany, showed otherwise. Actions like that of Lord Methuen against the entrenched Boers at Magersfontein in December 1899 showed once again that the frontal attack was doomed. As a result of their experiences the British finally threw off their old ideas. Infantry

11

were trained to appreciate the value of individual marksmanship and to think a little as individuals. Like the Germans the British introduced a closer tie-up between artillery and infantry, and the artillery were taught the technique of indirect fire, whereby the guns remained out of sight of the enemy and were controlled by forward observers. Yet again, as with the French, there was the same belief in the two stage battle. As *Infantry Training* (Volume 1 1914) put it: 'The action of the infantry in attack must therefore be considered as a constant pressing forward to close with the enemy. When effective ranges are reached there must usually be a fire fight, more or less prolonged according to the circumstances, in order to beat down the fire of the defenders. The leading lines will be reinforced and as the enemy's fire is gradually subdued, further progress will be made by bounds from place to place, the movement getting renewed force at each pause until the enemy can be assaulted with the bayonet.'

The future combatants had therefore resolved that the next war, when it came, must consist of one single battle. The enemy must be struck quickly before he had the chance to entrench. The tragedy was that no country's military leaders considered what would happen if the enemy were not decisively defeated in the opening stages and were allowed to entrench. It was left to a civilian, a Polish banker called Bloch, to foresee what would happen. He based his theory on the fact that: 'The outward and visible sign of the end of war was the evolution of the magazine rifle... The soldier by natural evolution has so perfected the mechanism of slaughter that he has practically secured his own extinction.' His picture of the next war, as he described it in 1897, proved frighteningly accurate: 'At first there will be increased slaughter – increased slaughter on so terrible a scale as to render it impossible to get troops to push the battle to decisive issue. They will try to, thinking that they are fighting under the old conditions, and they will learn such a lesson that they will abandon the attempt for ever. Then, instead of war being fought out to the bitter end in a series of decisive battles, we shall have as a substitute a long period of continuing strain upon the resources of the combatants. The war, instead of being a hand-to-hand contest, in which the combatants measure their physical and moral superiority, will become a kind of stalemate, in which neither army being willing to get at the other, both armies will be maintained in opposition to each other, threatening the other, but never being able to deliver the final and decisive attack.' He foresaw infantry being entrenched on both sides and that artillery would become the dominant arm. Yet, for all his accurate prophesying, he could not suggest a solution on the battlefield to the deadlock. Naval blockade was his answer and the country which had the superior navy and could impose this would win. Unfortunately virtually no notice was taken of his writings by the High Command of any of the combatants.

In their belief that war, when it came, must be over quickly, the plans of the two sides developed accordingly. The German Schlieffen Plan called for a massive wheel through Belgium and north-west France, passing to the west of Paris, by a force of some forty divisions. The French would then be defeated with their backs to their own frontier defences – and the whole operation was calculated to take no more than forty days. With the French defeated in the west they would then be able to set about the Russians at leisure. It was accepted that Belgian neutrality would have to be ignored for the plan to work, and Schlieffen in his original version wanted that of Holland to be disregarded as well. His successor, Moltke the younger, blanched at this and amended the plan to exclude

Alfred von Schlieffen. His plan, a sweep from the north through Belgium towards Paris, envisaged knocking France out of the war within forty days

Holland. The result of this was that the Germans would have to deal with the fortress of Liège before they could effectively get the plan into operation. Schlieffen had also deliberately kept the German left wing weak in order to encourage a French attack through Alsace and Lorraine, which France had ceded in 1871 and which had become a symbol of eventual revenge against Germany. This would take the French eye off events in the north. Moltke here again did not have the nerve to carry out Schlieffen's plan completely and strengthened his left at the expense of the right. Instead of falling back and drawing the French on, the German armies on the left were to stand where they were, and even to take the offensive, thereby creating a double envelopment.

The French plan, which was aimed at defeating a German invasion, also relied on the offensive. In 1905 Plan XV had favoured a preliminary defensive followed by a massive offensive, but Joffre, the French Commander-in-Chief at the start of the war, did not favour this and Plan XVII took its place. This was based on two premises, both of which were false: firstly, that the Germans would not employ reserves initially and therefore would not have the troops to attack in both Belgium and Lorraine; secondly, that *élan* made the French soldier irresistible in attack. Consequently it was resolved to attack between Mézières and Epinal and destroy the German centre, thereby, it was hoped, frustrating German designs from the start.

On 2nd August 1914 German troops poured across the border into Luxembourg and on the next day, after the formalities of an ultimatum had been observed, they were across into Belgium. Almost immediately they came up against the fortress of Liège and thanks to the resolute courage of General Leman, the Belgian commander, it was to be ten days before they could reduce it. The power of the defence had shown itself for the first time in the war. Meanwhile the French launched their planned attacks. The Battle of the Frontiers, as it was known, lasted for ten days. The French infantry, advancing in their blue coats and red trousers, as their forebears had a hundred years before, proved no match for the German artillery and machine-guns and suffered 300,000 casualties, thereby proving that *élan* was not enough to bring about victory. In spite of the superiority of the French '75' over the German 77mm the preponderance of German heavy artillery combined with superior methods of fire control meant that the French artillery were consistently outgunned. Meanwhile the great wheel in the north continued. On the 23rd the Germans came up against the British, who had taken up their position with four divisions on the left of the French at Mons. Once again the power of the defence was shown when the British managed to hold up six times their number. Prewar musketry training also paid off and the Germans believed that each British battalion was equipped with

13

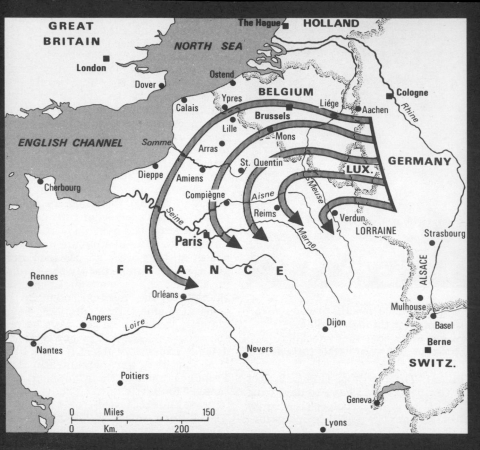

The Schlieffen Plan

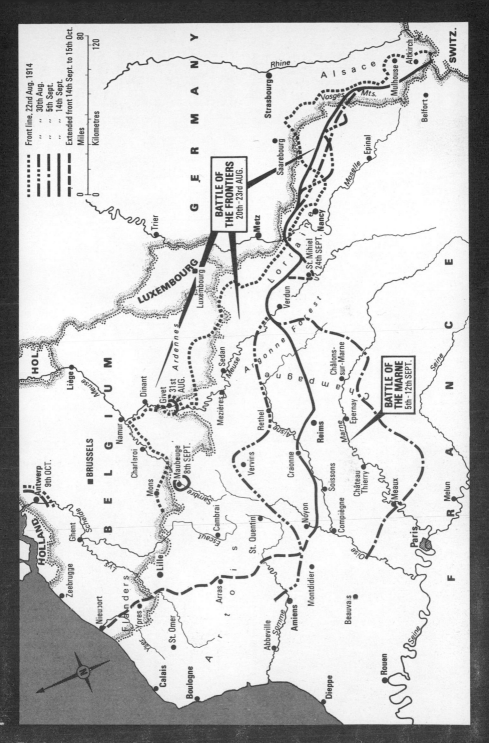

The German drive to Paris at the outbreak of the war

nothing but machine-guns, instead of a mere two in reality.

However, things were going wrong with the German plan. All had not gone well on the Eastern Front where the Russian offensive was initially showing success. In view of the resounding German victory during the Battle of the Frontiers, Moltke detached two corps and a cavalry division from his right wing to reinforce the Eastern Front. Another three corps had also been bottled up in observing the Belgian Army in Antwerp and laying siege to Maubeuge. Consequently the wheel had shrunk and now passed east of Paris instead of west of it. Matters had not been helped by the fact that Moltke had virtually lost control over his sub-ordinate commanders. The British had fallen back in retreat, but Joffre had hastily formed a fresh army, which took its place on the British left. On the 29th the French Fifth Army under Lanrezac, more by accident than design, caught the German wheel in the left flank and pushed it westwards, off course. The result, which was noticed by Allied air reconnaissance, was that the Germans were now enveloped on three sides. On 6th September the Allies turned and sent the German line, as far east as Verdun, reeling back. The Schlieffen Plan had, through misunderstanding and bad execution, failed.

By 12th September the miracle of the Marne had taken place and the German armies had halted on the Aisne in order to turn on their pursuers. Moltke was able to take up a defensive position on ground of his own choosing. The German armies dug

The German 7.7cm field gun. *Calibre:* 7.7cm. *Barrel length:* 27 calibres. *Weight of shell:* 15 lbs. *Weight of gun in action:* 1 ton. *Muzzle velocity:* 1,523 feet per second

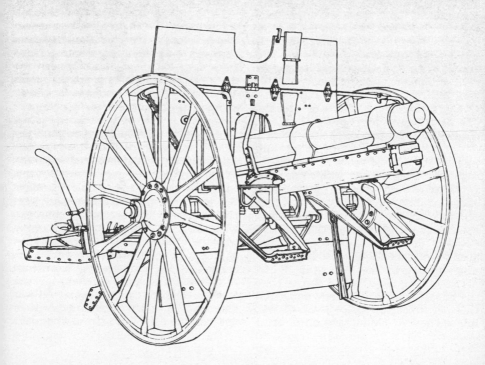

in on the high ground north of the Aisne and brought up a large amount of artillery support. The Allies, although they were able to get across the Aisne, came up against such strong defences, especially in the Chemin des Dames area, that it was only on the left, towards Compiègne, that they were able to make noticeable further progress. By the morning of 15th September Joffre had issued orders for the Allies to entrench where they stood. It was now clear that the pursuit phase had ended and only methodical set-piece attacks would dislodge the Germans.

For the next fortnight both sides were to have a foretaste of the type of warfare which was to dominate the Western Front for the next four years. The first thing to strike the combatants was that in the static conditions of the trenches artillery was the dominant weapon. One of Bloch's prophesies had come true. The Germans had the advantage of holding the higher ground. In addition, the British and French lacked heavy artillery, particularly howitzers, with the necessary elevation to take on the German positions on the heights. As a British Officer described it in his diary: 'The ordinary field trenches give sufficient protection from field gun shells, but not against the enemy's howitzer fire on our present fixed positions. Moreover, the Germans have brought up 8- and 11-inch howitzers which, outranging our lighter pieces, can fire without interruption.' The result was that the Allies were forced to dig deeper and deeper.

Related to the effect of artillery was the siting of the trenches themselves. Pre-war doctrine had accepted the need to entrench, but only as a temporary measure. The lessons of South Africa and Manchuria had shown that the effectiveness of defence depended on both cover and the volume of fire. Hence the British dug trenches, or at least rifle pits, before Mons and used their musketry training to very

telling effect. However trenches were dug with the emphasis of having a good field of fire for small arms. Yet a month after the Aisne Brigadier-General Montgomery was telling the British 8th Division in camp at Winchester that it was important that trenches were sited on reverse slopes and that a field of fire of no more than two to three hundred yards was necessary. As he said, 'whenever you find Germans in this war you will find them entrenched, and as a rule it means that sooner or later you are in a trench yourself and when you are entrenched down comes the fire of the big guns.' In other words, in order to outwit the enemy's artillery observers one's own positions must be out of their view. This is supported by an official publication, *Notes From the Front* Part II 1914, which stated 'trenches should . . . be sited having regard to possible "observation stations" on ground occupied by the enemy, and not solely with regard to the possible artillery positions of the enemy.'

To counter this new concept of siting trenches air artillery spotting was developed. The Germans had been using this method of reconnaissance from very early on and Joffre in his GQG Instruction 2083 of 24th August directed that the French artillery should use aircraft for the location of targets and direction of fire. British attempts at air spotting began unofficially and were pioneered on the Aisne on 8th September by two young officers of the Royal Flying Corps, Lieutenants D S Lewis and B T James. However, both sides realised that their artillery was not really equipped with the right ammunition for trench warfare. Shrapnel, although very effective against troops in the open, caused little damage to trenches. High explosive ammunition was the answer, but at the outbreak of war this made up only eleven per cent of the French stocks and twenty per cent of the German. The British were in a worse position in that it was reserved

Above: Early British trenches on the Aisne after the miracle of the Marne had halted the German onslaught. No sign yet of barbed wire. *Below:* German heavy howitzers. Superiority in heavy artillery gave the Germans a critical advantage in the early days on the Western Front

solely for their few heavier artillery pieces.

Another result of the accuracy of the German artillery fire was spy mania. Both the French and British became convinced that there was a vast network of spies operating within their lines on the Aisne. Almost every account of the battle mentions this and *The Times* of 29th September carried a long report on their supposed activities. Undoubtedly there were some spies operating, but not in the numbers that reports of the time would have one believe, and it is highly likely that their work led to the death of innocent civilians. The Allies failed to grasp the fact that much of the Germans' artillery success was caused by good observation from their positions on the high ground.

Meanwhile, attacks launched from the trenches by both sides had little success, and exhaustion and lack of reserves caused them merely to dig deeper and sit tighter in order to lick their wounds and recover their breath. The Allied press was content to give the armies a pat on the back for the fact that their 'steel wall' had held against repeated German counter-attacks, forgetting that the Germans had been the more successful in that they had been able to recover from the disasters on the Marne. The Allied generals, however, were fully conscious of the need to push on and again we turn to General Montgomery's talk to illustrate something of the anxiety of the Allied High Command. '. . . You must do something to save your infantry from this nerve-racking work in the trenches and at the same time be preparing for your forward movement. You must not remain absolutely on the passive defensive . . . I think our tendency has been rather too much digging into these trenches and being satisfied to stay there. There has not been enough effort to move ahead and look forward to the time when we have got to push on.' This feeling was to remain particu-

Von der Marwitz. His race to the sea to outflank the Allies had failed by mid-October; the war of movement was over, and only headlong frontal attacks could break the deadlock

larly with the British General Staff for the rest of the war and explains why British trenches were always less secure and not so well constructed as those of their opponents.

By the end of the first week of October the Germans had realised that their only chance of achieving a 'knock-out' blow lay in trying to outflank the Allied armies from the north. Consequently during the first ten days of October a series of attacks took place, moving gradually northwards. Three German corps launched an attack against Arras and struck the French Tenth Army on 2nd October. Although the French lost ground they managed to prevent a breakthrough and by the 9th another forty-five miles of line had become permanent. Meanwhile Marwitz and three cavalry corps started to sweep through Flanders with the aim of getting at the Allied rear and blocking all railway communications from the coast towards Paris. However, the French territorials opposing him

20

managed to put up a stout resistance for long enough to enable Legrand-Girarde's crack XXI Corps to mount a counterattack from Béthune. This almost cut through the German cavalry and was only frustrated in turn by the arrival of German XIV Corps, which had arrived at Mons from Metz on the 6th. Marwitz was now ordered to try again further north between La Bassée and Armentières. Meanwhile his right-hand corps under Lieutenant-General von Hollen had succeeded in entering Ypres on the 8th and now headed towards Hazebrouck some twenty miles south-west in order to cut the Allied communications. Again, however, the French managed to block this attempt with a hastily improvised cavalry corps of two divisions under de Mitry, and by the end of the 8th Hollen was retiring on Bailleul.

At the same time the BEF had been switched from their positions on the Aisne and were now deploying themselves on the La Bassée-Aire canal,

Belgian infantry, showing the strain of retreat, in front of Ypres, October 1914. Neither side yet realised it, but with the First Battle of Ypres the war of attrition had begun

linking up with the French under de Castlenau at Béthune. This was as a result of a suggestion made by the French to Joffre some ten days before. With Smith-Dorrien's II Corps taking on this task Pulteney's III Corps debouched from Hazebrouck in order to cover Smith-Dorrien on his left. Allenby and the cavalry, even further to the north, managed to establish themselves at Messines by the end of the 14th. On the same day they had managed to make contact with Rawlinson's IV Corps, which had arrived at Ypres after taking part in the unsuccessful attempt to prevent the Germans from taking Antwerp. The Belgians, following in Rawlinson's wake, were also falling back on the Nieuport-Dixmude line. Sir John French, the British commander, was

General Rawlinson, commander of
British IV Corps at Ypres

now trying to push forward against
Marwitz, but on the 15th the latter
was reinforced by two territorial
infantry divisions. The next three
days saw repeated British attacks,
but they were not able to advance
further than the River Lys. De Mitry,
now strengthened to four divisions,
filled the gap between Ypres and the
Belgians and the Allies now finally
managed to establish a continuous
defence line right up to the coast.
The 18th saw the last German attempt
to outflank with Duke Albrecht of
Württemberg's untrained volunteers
thrusting themselves in vain against
the Belgian defences on the Yser. The
race to the sea, which had started with
mere attempts to outflank, had
taken place over a distance of some
one hundred miles and it could be said
that it ended in a dead heat, or at least
stalemate. It was now obvious to both
sides that the war of movement was
over for the time being and that only
headlong frontal attacks, the very
manoeuvre that modern weapons had

shown to be fatal, provided a chance
to break the deadlock.

The attacks on the Yser on the 18th
heralded the start of the First Battle
of Ypres. It is a popular misconception
to imagine First Ypres as purely a
defensive battle as far as the Allies
were concerned. In the event, the
Allies believed that they had just as
much chance of punching a hole
through the German defences, which
they believed to be non-existent
between Lille and Antwerp. Although
the French had not the troops to put
into the attack on this part of the
front, the British had been bolstered
with the arrival of Haig's I Corps
from the south and the Indian Corps.
The opening of the battle was virtually a headlong clash between the
opposing advancing troops. True, air
reconnaissance had warned Sir John
French that he could expect stiffer
opposition in the shape of Württemberg's reserve divisions, which were
now on their way from Lille. The
German cavalry in front of the British

troops acted merely as a screen, which helped to disguise the intentions of the advancing Germans.

It is convenient to split the battle into four phases and in this first, which lasted up to the 21st October, the German Fourth and, south of it, Sixth Army steadily pushed the Allies back north and south of Ypres. This produce the immortal Ypres Salient, which was to become the British Verdun for the remainder of the war. The other three phases cover the major German attacks on the salient. Phase two started with an attempt by Foch, who had started the war as a corps commander and had now been placed in charge of the whole of the Allied northern sector, to regain the initiative. Dubois's IX Corps was brought up as reinforcement, but did not arrive in the line until after the intended time for launching the attack. All that were available were de Mitry's two hard-worked cavalry divisions and requests at the last moment to Haig for co-

German reserves move on Ypres

operation from his corps were fruitless since he was already mounting a successful local counterattack of his own. Hence the idea of an offensive came to nothing and it became possible for the British I Corps to be relieved by Dubois and to be set aside as a much needed reserve. The Germans now concentrated their attacks in two sectors. In the north Württemberg tackled Dixmude, which was defended by French sailors and Belgian infantry. Preceded by a steady artillery bombardment, attacks were launched throughout the 25th. Dixmude held, although north of it the Germans under Besseler managed to penetrate to the Dixmude-Nieuport railway on the Allied side of the Yser. In the centre on the same day three of Württemberg's corps, made up of volunteers with incomplete military training, attacked Dubois, who managed to gain some ground with a counterattack. However in the south

23

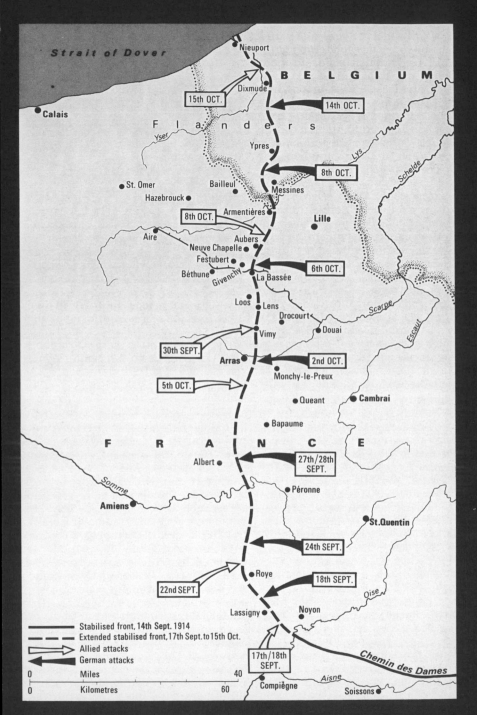

The Race to the Sea : Allied and German attempts to outflank each other

the German Fourth Army made a determined effort against Capper's 7th British Division. They managed to punch a hole around the village of Reutel, but luckily did not press their advantage and there was time for Haig to send in the 2nd Division to plug the gap.

Phase three was heralded by a thirty-six hour bombardment by the Germans and throughout the period 26th-29th they attacked again and again. Somehow the line managed to hold and reinforcements were starting to trickle into the Salient. The Germans then tried again on the 31st and launched their last available reserves north-west between Messines and the little village of Gheluvelt on the Ypres-Menin Road. Haig's I Corps broke and his two divisional commanders became casualties to the same shell. All seemed lost until a single battalion, the 2nd Worcesters, launched a desperate counterattack on Gheluvelt Chateau, which miraculously stopped the German attack. As John Terraine has written: 'it was the last time that such a handful would be able to produce such an effect – the last flourish of the old British Regular tradition.' There was now a lull of sorts and Haig had time to construct a new defence line. The final phase began on 10th November when the Germans finally managed to take Dixmude, but it benefitted them little as the Belgians had let in the sea at Nieuport and flooded the banks of the Yser. The next day produced the final flourish with a newly constituted force under Linsingen, consisting of crack divisions brought up from the south. Again they concentrated on the Menin Road and, having captured Hill 60 from a French brigade, fell on the British in the Gheluvelt area. Held in Gheluvelt itself the 1st Guards Division managed to penetrate the British trenches to the north, but were slowed up on coming in contact with Haig's defence line to the rear. General FitzClarence's Brigade counterattacked them in Polygon

Haig (British I Corps), who bore the brunt of the crisis at Ypres, with Rawlinson. After Ypres the trench line was virtually continuous from Switzerland to the sea

Wood and the battle was over.

Stalemate had now been reached and there was no further chance of either side gaining a decisive victory in 1914. The scar across the countryside from Switzerland to the sea was now a reality and trench warfare had come to stay. The First Battle of Ypres is thus highly significant for this and many other reasons.

It made the Germans realise that overwhelming numbers were not enough to carry the day. The slaughter of those six reserve corps came to be known as the *Kindermord bei Ypern* – 'The Massacre of the Innocents at Ypres'. Advancing in closely packed ranks, like the armies of old, they were no match for entrenched determined regular troops with their high standards of musketry. The German artillery had far outnumbered the Allied guns in quantity and weight. Yet again it had been proved that with determination it was possible to survive its effects. The British developed the tactic of evacuating their front line trenches during a bombardment, which undoubtedly saved casualties, but was risky – it was this practice that enabled the Germans to penetrate on the final day of the battle.

Allied co-operation, which went through good and bad stages, was never higher than here. Dubois, in particular, had his troops everywhere reinforcements were needed. It was the graveyard of the old British regular army. 'The old army died so gloriously at Ypres because the battle they had to fight called for those qualities of unflinching courage and dogged self-sacrifice in which they were pre-eminent' as C S Forester in his novel *The General* put it. Two thirds of the troops engaged met with death or wounds and this was to have far reaching effects on Kitchener's New Armies, which were in the process of being raised at home.

The battle also produced the idea that ground must be held at all costs. Troops had gone into the battle and dug their individual rifle pits where they stood. These pits were gradually connected into trenches. Orders from above, because of the gravity of the situation, especially with the extreme lack of reserves, necessarily had to be short and to the point. 'Defence to the last man' was the cry and this meant holding one's ground to the last, however badly positioned one might be from the tactical point of view. The sheer psychological effect of being allowed to withdraw to more favourable ground would have led to unnecessary withdrawals, which might have lost the battle. Regular troops would accept this; their training was geared to obeying orders unquestioningly. As a result the commanders developed a phobia against giving up ground, which was to lead to unfortunate incidents later on, especially with conscripted troops. The Germans never followed this idea so closely. But neither the French, (because they would never voluntarily give up more acres of *La Belle Patrie*)

Individual rifle pits, the first stage in trench construction

nor the British (because it simply was not done) would ever have contemplated withdrawals such as the Germans were to carry out later in the war. As a result, as we shall see, in many places along the front the Germans were allowed to be left in possession of the pick of the ground.

As to the combatants themselves, in the words of the British Official History, '. . . there was now nothing to do but to lie at the bottom of the trenches and in the holes in the ground, which, when they had a few planks, a door, or some branches, and a few inches of earth over them, were in those days called "dug-outs".'

The Cloth Hall at Ypres, showing the effect of the German bombardment

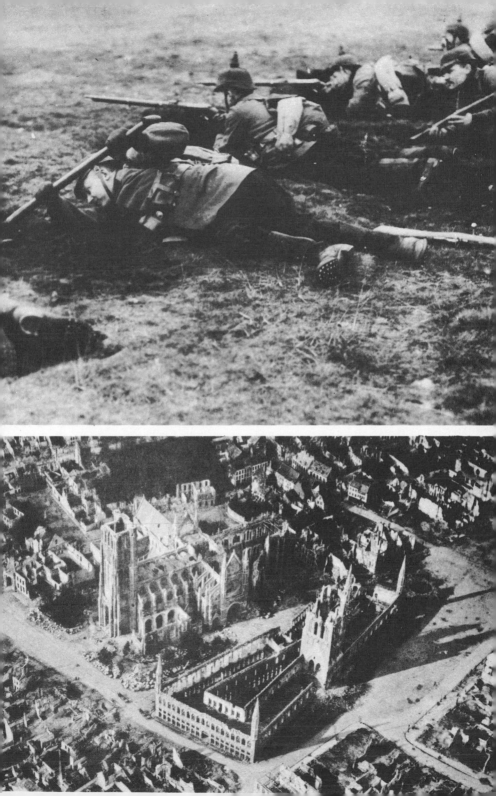

The close season 1914-1915

By the time the First Battle of Ypres had ended, the war in the west had been going on for three months. There had been little respite and the casualties on both sides were enormous. The initial mobilisation stocks of ammunition were exhausted and the surviving troops were urgently in need of rest. The wintry weather was closing in and it was time to go into 'Winter Quarters'.

Before going any further it would be as well to take a trip along the trenches and look at the terrain. By mid-November the trench system ran in an unbroken line for some 475 miles from Switzerland to the North Sea. It can be likened to a shallow 'S', which has been tilted backwards. From Nieuport on the coast the front ran down along the flooded Yser, which forced both sides to build up rather than dig down, to Dixmude and thence on round the Ypres salient until the French frontier was reached north-west of Armentières. In the coastal strip the country was entirely flat. Around Ypres there was high ground, but never more than sixty metres above sea level. Most of this was held by the Germans, in particular Hill 60, two miles south-west of Ypres, and the Wytschaete-Messines Ridge to the south. These features might seem to be insignificant as regards height, but because of the general lowness of the ground they really did dominate the surrounding countryside. This lowness also created the additional problem that water was never far below ground.

From Armentières, which lay just inside the Allied lines, the trenches ran down through Givenchy and Lens; a dull mining area dotted with slag-heaps, which provided good observation positions. South of here the country changed radically and gave way to rolling chalk ridges commencing in the north with what was to become the celebrated Vimy Ridge (in German hands at this stage). Down through Arras and then across the marshy lowlands of the Somme

Above and below: Opposing German and French trenches on the Marne, 1914-1915.
Even at this date the Germans were digging deeper than the French

Above: A trench in the Argonne, 1914 – very different to the orderly layout prescribed in the official manuals. *Below left:* The King of the Belgians, commander of the Belgian army's six weak divisions. *Below right:* 'Papa' Joffre. In the popular imagination he came to be seen as the saviour of France in 1914

Valley to just north of Compiègne, where the line turned eastwards along the line of the Aisne. The Germans here continued to hold the high ground to the north of the river and the heights to the north of Reims, the line having crossed the Aisne just south of Craonne. The trenches now cut through the French army's peacetime training area, named the *Champagne Pouilleuse*, and thence into the forests of the Argonne, an area of broken hilly country. The River Meuse was cut in two places, north and south of the ancient fortress of Verdun, which dominated the heights above the river. This created another notable salient. South of Verdun the Germans had a similar salient across the Meuse about St Mihiel. The front now fell away more and more southwards across the Vosges Mountains and thence across the Belfort Gap to meet the Swiss frontier below Altkirch.

It very quickly became clear that a large part of the front was going to be unsuitable for major operations. South of Verdun little was to happen throughout the war and the extreme northern coastal strip was likewise inactive. From Ypres down to the Argonne activity was to remain at a constant high level, although only in the downlands north of the Somme was the ground really suitable for offensive action.

The remnants of the Belgian army, consisting of some six weak divisions under the command of their king, held the strip from the coast down to Dixmude. Then came two French Corps, IX and XX, who covered from Dixmude to Ypres. The British sector ran from St Eloi, near Ypres, down to La Bassée, a distance in terms of the actual trench line of twenty-eight miles. This was held by ten British infantry divisions and two Indian. Besides this were three British cavalry divisions, who were being used in a dismounted role and two Indian cavalry divisions. The remainder of the front was held by some eighty French divisions. Opposing them were 106 German divisions which were to be run down to 98 by the beginning of 1915, on account of transfers to the Eastern Front. Thus both sides were in approximately equal strength.

The dying down of the Battle of Ypres did not mean that both sides went into hibernation, the traditional meaning of going into winter quarters. Activity did not noticeably decrease. For a start Joffre wanted to be able to be in a position to defeat the invader as early as possible in 1915. He was urged on by Foch, who in a report to Joffre on the 19th November wrote that: 'The German plan has failed, better still, we ourselves are in perfect condition, both morally and materially, for attacking them.' In this report he saw the necessity for ' . . . a large number of siege guns, with plenty of ammunition'. He emphasised the need for engineers and grenades and prophetically suggested that the German defences should be mined and heavy charges exploded under them. In conclusion he foresaw offensive operations as being ' . . . against fortified positions, in other words siege warfare on a vast scale'. The Allies were ill-equipped for trench warfare. The Germans had the stocks of mortars, heavy artillery and grenades because they had been prepared for siege warfare in having to capture the Belgian frontier forts before the Schlieffen Plan could be put into operation.

Unfortunately Foch's ideas, although sound and realistic, were not fully understood by Joffre, who was impatient for quick victories. He decided on two major attacks, one at Arras and one in Champagne, with subsidiary attacks elsewhere along the front. His orders showed his concept of operations as being ' . . . not only to push the enemy towards the northeast, but to cut his communications with Germany'. But the armies were given only a week to prepare and the offensives were a disaster. The Arras

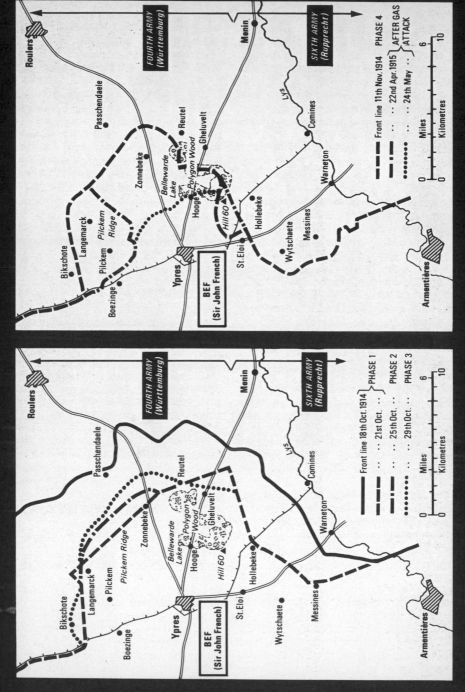

First and Second Ypres, showing the ever-shrinking salient

attack ground to a halt after six days on the 23rd December, and the Champagne attack launched on the 20th merely resulted in the capture of some front-line trenches. The reasons for failure were quickly apparent. Bad weather had turned the battlefields to mud and consequently slowed the advancing infantry right down – a problem that was to overshadow operations throughout the war on the Western Front. The attacks were uncoordinated and this gave the Germans time to recover between each attack. Finally, lack of artillery did more than anything to bring the offensive grinding to a halt. Joffre echoed Foch's words in his final report on the operations dated 17th March 1915. 'It was a matter of real siege operations against trenches with comprehensive defences – covered emplacements, armoured gun turrets, powerfully protected flanking emplacements'.

Joffre had hoped that a subsidiary attack by d'Urbal's army with the co-operation of the neighbouring BEF on the Wytschaete-Hollebeke sector would assist his attack north of Arras. The British however were still exhausted after their trials at Ypres and keenly felt their lack of trench warfare materials. They attacked rather halfheartedly around Wytschaete, where minor gains were made before the attack fizzled out, and then on the 18th December the Indian Corps attempted another in the Givenchy area, again without success. This brought down a German counter-attack two days later, which captured trenches on the northern outskirts of Givenchy. All along the front the fighting died down in preparation for the first Christmas of the war. Regrettably the failure of the British attacks had given the French the opinion that the British army '. . . might be helpful to hold the line and act defensively, but would be of little use to drive the

Germans on the Eastern Front celebrate the first Christmas of the war

A mechanical drainage pump at work on the British front during the winter of 1914-1915

Germans out of France'. An unfortunate opinion, which did little to inspire mutual confidence among the Allies.

Both sides now accepted that they had to live in their trenches for at least the next few weeks. To the Germans this was a godsend, and hence the move to transfer eight divisions to the Eastern Front in order to try to achieve a quick victory there. The first problem was to make the trenches habitable. In the south this was not such a problem, as firm ground and the availability of plenty of wood meant defence and comfort could be quickly achieved. The main problem was the lowlands north of Arras. The Germans, occupying, as they did, most of the high ground, were able to keep their trenches drained and hence reasonably dry. For the British this was the first obstacle to overcome. 'Within twenty-four hours there was "rain, rain, rain".

The winter floods had come, the ditch turned out to be a stream which opened into the river; it was one of the main drains in this much-drained low country. The parapet fell in right and left; the ditch-trench ran with a rapid current, and had to be abandoned by day'. This experience of the 2nd Royal Welsh Fusiliers is typical. At the time of First Ypres the many ditches intersecting the countryside were obvious places to take up defensive positions. By the end of the battle they were permanent parts of the front line and only the rains of early December made their inhabitants realise that they were, in fact, part of the intricate drainage system designed to combat the heavy rainfall for which Flanders was renowned. In this instance the Royal Welsh were lucky to have a saw-mill at hand with unlimited supplies of wood. This enabled them to shore up the trench and revet it; it remained one of the driest trenches in the sector. Most other units were not so lucky and had to rely on continuous teams of human balers and mechanically unreliable pumping systems.

Bruce Bairnsfather, an infantryman and creator of those cartoon characters 'Ole Bill' and 'Young Bert', who did more than most to keep up the morale of the BEF during the early days of trench warfare, has left us with a humourous description of what it was like. 'Select a flat ten-acre ploughed field, so sited that all the surface water of the surrounding country drains into it. Now cut a zig-zag slot about four feet deep and three feet wide diagonally across, dam off as much water as you can so as to leave about a hundred yards of squelchy mud; delve out a hole at one side of the slot, then endeavour to live there for a month on bully beef and damp biscuits, whilst a friend has instructions to fire at you with his Winchester every time you put your head above the surface.' To this might be added the continuous rain of trench mortar bombs, of which the Germans seemed to have unlimited quantities. The Allies had none, save home-made constructions, which were as lethal to the firer as to the enemy.

Surprisingly enough, both health and morale remained high in these conditions. Perhaps it was the active outdoor life. The main complaints were 'trench foot' and lice. Trench foot was caused by exposing the feet too long to cold water. They turned blue or red and became a mass of chilblains; in extreme cases gangrene set in. At the beginning no cure was laid down and it became a test of resourcesfulness of unit medical officers. Frequent foot inspections became a part of every junior officer's life and great emphasis was placed on frequent changes of socks and the use of grease or whale oil. This was another problem which was to remain throughout the war and the efficiency of a unit could be judged

Despite the terrible conditions which produced trench foot and lice, morale and health remained high during the first winter

by the number of its men admitted to hospital with this complaint. 'To be lousy with' was a First War expression meaning 'to be crawling with'. Every front-line soldier experienced lice. Having to wear the same clothes for days on end brought them out in no time. Their eggs were quickly incubated with body heat. Bath houses were established behind the lines and every man on coming out of the trenches was given a hot bath and a change of shirt and underclothes. A more serious effect of lice was 'trench fever'. This had the symptoms of normal influenza and typhoid and, although it was seldom fatal, victims were incapacitated for a long time. It was not until 1918 that it was discovered that it was transmitted by the excreta of the louse.

Trench systems were now starting to adopt a recognised pattern. No Man's Land was anything from 25 to 500 yards across, although the average was more like 200–300 yards. Strands of cattlewire started to appear in front of the forward trenches. This was initially in single strands. It was hung with empty food tins and had the dual purpose of giving warning of the enemy approach by night and of preventing the enemy from throwing grenades into the forward trenches; it was always positioned over grenade-throwing distance from the forward trenches. No Man's Land itself soon became a litter of empty ration tins, dead bodies, and shell holes. Instead of being in the traditional straight line trenches were constructed as a series of traverses, which, from the air, gave a castellated appearance. This prevented enfilade fire from the flanks. In the northern part of the line, because of the damp conditions, it became necessary to build up breastworks rather than attempt to dig downwards. Stretching back from the front line were a number of communication trenches, again constructed in a zigzag shape to prevent enfilade fire. These ran back to a support trench and thence through to a reserve line.

This was the British idea in theory. In practice the actual layout at the front seemed to bear little relation to the copybook systems which were being dug up by the embryonic New Armies on the training areas of Salisbury Plain and elsewhere. The main problem was lack of labour, a shortage that the French did not suffer from.

By contrast with the British, the French believed that the front line should not be held in strength, since this brought unnecessary casualties. Instead they had a system of alternating active and passive zones. Active zones consisted of fortified strongpoints with the ability to fire both to the front and to the flanks. This flanking fire gave cover to the passive zones, which were heavily wired and manned merely by a few sentries. Behind these was a line of strongpoints, designed to be shellproof in order to accommodate the support companies. Finally two miles to the rear there was constructed a 'stop line' similar to the front line to counter local breakthroughs. The Germans had a different concept yet again. They believed in a heavily defended single line with a subsidiary series of concrete machine-gun emplacements constructed some thousand yards to the rear.

Trench warfare quickly fell into a routine. On the British front a brigade of four infantry battalions would have two in the trenches and two in support, normally being billeted in villages and farms some two miles behind the line. Each reserve battalion would have one company on immediate standby to reinforce the trenches in an emergency. The two forward battalions had two companies forward and two in the reserve trenches. The two forward companies each had two platoons forward and two back in the support trenches. Each battalion was responsible for something like 800–1,000 yards of frontage and given that the average strength of a platoon was forty men this gave a density of one rifle per five yards in the front line. This was the ideal, but in the winter of 1914–1915 lack of reserves often meant that the frontages were more like 1,200–1,500 yards and that battalions had to have all four companies up forward. This was not caused so much by battalions themselves being under strength, as by the many other tasks, besides merely defending the front line, which took away manpower.

For obvious reasons, it was always safer to move about at night and so, very quickly, as far as routine work went, night was turned into day. Brigadier-General James Jack, who fought throughout the war on the Western Front as an infantry officer, gives a good idea of the sort of tasks that had to be done. The time is December 1914. 'The duties were very heavy. Construction and maintenance of wire entanglements as well as earthworks, the finding of sentries and parties to carry up rations besides other stores, engaged fully two-thirds of all ranks throughout every night. Half the trench garrison performed repair work for at least three hours during daylight.' The two battalions in reserve had to provide large working parties every night to go up the line either as carrying parties or to assist the engineers in constructing or improving defences. This practice of using troops supposedly at rest was to be a bone of contention with the front-line soldiers throughout the war. The French had life better organised and tended to employ their more elderly territorials for this type of task, thus giving their actual fighting troops more chance to rest.

Two other front-line tasks added to the steady trickle of casualties suffered, even during the quieter times. Patrolling of No Man's Land was the first. Both sides sent out small parties every night to learn what they could of the enemy opposite. How strongly held were his trenches? What was his system of reliefs? What damage had our artillery fire done? These were the sort of questions which had to be answered. Sometimes opposing patrols bumped into one another in the dark; a brief exchange of shots, the odd yell, and both patrols were scampering back to their own lines. This tended to be the signal for a general interchange of fire along the whole sector; 'wind-up', it was called by the British. This led to a general stand-to and both sides waited alert for a possible attack until the firing once again died down. The troops in the front line always stood-to as a matter of course for an hour at both dusk and dawn, as these were the most likely times for an attack to be launched. It was occasionally possible to ambush an enemy patrol and to capture a prisoner – naturally a valuable source of Intelligence – was looked on as a great achievement. Patrolling was the main method of dominating No Man's Land and it helped to foster the offensive spirit which was so necessary if major attacks were to be successful.

Much of the repair work on the trenches was done in order to make them secure enough to provide good 'jump-off' positions for the spring offensives. There was also the necessity of preventing the enemy from achieving this, which need brought about the first trench raid of the war. The Indian Corps and more especially the 1/39th and 2/39th Gerhwal Rifles can claim responsibility for this. They were having trouble with a German trench which was enfilading their lines. On the night of 9/10th November a party of fifty men from each battalion raided it and tried to destroy it. They found it too well constructed to be knocked out more than temporarily and had to make another attempt three nights later which resulted in casualties and failed, because of the alertness of the Germans. This, however, set the pattern for a type of local operation which was to become more and more frequent as the war progressed. It was another means of dominating No Man's Land and became very much a favourite of the British. The Germans were to use it quite often, but the French never really took to it until the last few

Sir John French, C-in-C of the British
Expeditionary Force

months of the war.

The first really successful raid was
carried out on the night of the 2/3rd
January 1915 by Lieutenant F C Roberts and twenty-five men of the 1st
Worcesters who succeeded in bayonet-
ting a large party of Germans who had
dug a trench to within fifty yards of
the British line at Pont Logy in the
Neuve Chapelle sector. Roberts was
immediately awarded the Distin-
guished Service Order and later in the
war was to win the Victoria Cross and
Military Cross. General Jack had
nearly found himself engaged on a
similar venture on 22nd December,
but it was, to his relief, cancelled. By

the end of January the Germans had
also taken up this new tactic in a
series of raids against the British 27th
and 28th Divisions, both comparatively new to the front, in the St Eloi
sector. The pattern of a raid had
become clear. Whereas a local attack
had the object of capturing enemy
positions, a raid was a means of
entering the enemy's trenches to capture prisoners, inflict casualties and
destroy emplacements before return-
ing to the safety of one's own lines.

In certain fields urgent rethinking
was needed. None of the combatants
had envisaged that there would be so
much demand for artillery. Consequently by December 1914 all were
desperately short of artillery ammunition. None felt this more seriously

Communications, too, needed re-organising. The traditional methods of signalling, runner, flag and heliograph were not suitable for trench warfare. The artillery, whose efficiency relied on the ability of observers to transmit information about the location of targets and the correction of fire back to the guns, used telephone and line. It was therefore decided that the infantry should also adopt this as the main system of communication. For the Germans the decision did not create a problem, as their pre-war establishments allowed for telephones down to battalion headquarters and they consequently already had unit signallers trained in this medium. For the British and French, who initially had line only down to regimental or brigade (British) headquarters, it meant, however, that battalion signallers had to be completely retrained. Nevertheless by early 1915 they had succeeded in running lines down to company HQs. At the same time improvements were being made in air-ground communications for artillery spotting. By the end of 1914 three methods were in use, flare, lamp and wireless. The early aircraft wirelesses were very heavy and took up the whole of the observer's seat, which meant that the pilot had to fly, navigate, spot and send messages all at the same time; a difficult operation at the best of times and even more so with the primitive aircraft of the time. Efforts were therefore made to reduce the size of these wireless sets so that the observer could be carried.

The winter of 1914–15 was regarded by both sides as merely a breathing space. They realised that the war on the Western Front was no more than a gigantic siege operation, but felt that this was merely a temporary phase. With the coming of the spring, the enemy's line would be breached and once again warfare would become open. In the meantime the static conditions gave the combatants the chance to show off their ingenuity.

than the British. Sir John French estimated in December 1914 that the requirement per day for each 18-pounder field gun was fifty rounds. In December only six rounds per gun were being produced and this was to drop even further in January to under five rounds per day. As we shall see, this was to produce a severe brake on the British offensive effort in 1915. Suffice it to say, in the meantime British artillery was very strictly rationed, sometimes to as little as three rounds per day while larger calibres had as few as one round. This was at a time when artillery support was urgently required to prevent the German positions from becoming too strong, and so reduce their chances of success in the spring.

First steps

At the start of the New Year both sides were found wrestling with the problem of how to break the deadlock on the Western Front. The British were perturbed by the whole idea of accepting a 'siege war' and put forward suggestions for tackling the problem in a different way. On 2nd January Lord Kitchener wrote to Sir John French: 'I suppose we must now recognise that the French army cannot make a sufficient break through the German lines to bring about the retreat of the German forces in northern France. If that is so, then the German lines in France may be looked upon as a fortress that cannot be carried by assault and also that cannot be completely invested, with the result that the lines may be held by an investing force, whilst operations proceed elsewhere.' This view was strongly supported by Churchill, as First Lord of the Admiralty, and by Lloyd George, who was then Minister of Munitions.

The first idea was for an outflanking operation along the Belgian Coast. An army with strong naval support would advance up the coast and seize the Belgian ports as far as Zeebrugge. This was agreed to by Sir John French, but was turned down by Joffre, who felt that the operations for 1915 must have the clearcut purpose of ridding France and all or part of Belgium of the invader. The second originated in a paper written by Colonel Maurice Hankey, Secretary of the Committee for Imperial Defence. Nicknamed 'The Boxing Day Memo', it put forward the idea that an attack should be made on Turkey and a Balkan alliance with Greece and Bulgaria organised for this venture. Hankey saw no reason why three army corps could not be diverted from the Western Front to support this campaign. The scheme was eagerly snatched up by Churchill and Lloyd George, who went further in suggesting that the bulk of the British

A German ammunition party in the Champagne, early 1915

forces be transferred to the Balkans to bolster up hard pressed Serbia. However, these grandiose schemes met with strong opposition from Joffre, who was supported by French. What became known as the struggle between the Easterners and Westerners was to be waged bitterly for the rest of the war. The ideas originated by Hankey were put into action, but only in very emasculated form, in the expeditions to the Dardanelles and Salonika. The truth of the matter was that it was French territory, not British, which had been invaded and occupied. The French were, at that time, bearing the major burden of the Allied effort on the Western Front and quite naturally had the louder voice in affairs. Understandably they wanted first priority to be given to ridding French territory of the German invader. There was also the argument that Germany's strength lay in her army and that to defeat her meant beating her army in the field. While the bulk of that army continued to remain on the Western Front the major part of the Allied effort must also be employed there in order to provide the best chance of succeeding in this.

There was no such dissension in the German ranks. Their plan for 1915 was quite simple; to contain the enemy in the west whilst they went for a quick victory against the Russians in the east.

Early in February Joffre issued his offensive plan. It was a continuation of the preparatory attacks of December 1914 and envisaged converging blows from Artois and Champagne on the great salient formed by the German front. At the same time an attack would be launched through Lorraine in order to threaten the German communications. The British contribution was to be a synchronised attack against La Bassée in support of the northern attack. Joffre also wanted Sir John French to take over the sector manned by the French IX Corps north of Ypres, but Sir John demurred and relations between the two became

De Langle de Cary, commander of the French Fourth Army whose assault in the Champagne ground to a halt in March 1915

more strained. Joffre postponed his own northern attack because he could not have the IX Corps and invited the British 'to go it alone'.

De Langle de Cary's Fourth French Army, which had carried out the Champagne operations of December, had continued to press the Germans in the same area until after the middle of January. Rain, defective artillery ammunition and the exhaustion of the troops themselves had finally brought offensive operations to a halt. Joffre now ordered him to renew the offensive, stipulating that attacks must be preceded by heavier artillery barrages and that a strong second line of trenches must be dug in order to prevent any German counterattack breaking through the French lines.

On 25th January de Langle de Cary reported to Joffre on the plans he had made for renewing the offensive. His main deduction from a study of his previous failures was that separate attacks by individual corps on narrow

fronts was unsatisfactory, not so much because of the lack of synchronisation, but more because there was not room enough to push reserves through the narrow breaches which had been made. Hence he decided to attack on a wider front. It was, however, essential to await drier weather to give the attacking troops greater mobility. Joffre agreed and in the meantime preparations for the attack were put under way. This entailed the construction of the second line and the improvement of the front line, local attacks being mounted in some places to improve 'jump-off' positions. French preparations were much hindered by determined German counterattacks and the steady deterioration of the weather, which prompted General Brulard of the 2nd Division to report on 2nd February that: 'Fieldworks have been stopped by the beginning of the thaw. First line units can only clean up the trenches where they stand knee-deep in water. We did manage over a five day period to ensure the revictualling of the regiments in the front line. Men and animals are under excessive strain which cannot be accepted any longer as it is leading to a wastage we cannot afford.' More reserves had to be brought up and the offensive did not finally get under way until 12th February. It was to carry on for more than a month until the men's exhaustion finally proved too much for them. The German defence system of mutually supporting strongpoints, together with their capacity for immediate counterattack, prevented anything more than the most minor successes. In fact by the end the French had given up all ideas of frontal assault and were relying on infiltration techniques. Unfortunately, de Lange de Cary, in his report on the fighting, did not stress the possibilities for infiltration. He contented himself by saying that 'the offensive . . . made it quite clear that it is possible for a mass of five or six army corps to live, move and fight in a limited area with neither roads nor shelters,

French lorry-drawn 120mm guns;
obsolete, but better than nothing

and where the thaw had turned the few roads and tracks into mud, on which it required 16 horses to haul an ammunition wagon up to the guns.' Joffre felt that it had taken the strain off the remainder of the front, had prevented any German offensive from taking place, and shown that 'our troops in the zone of advance have an obvious superiority in morale'. Reality is sometimes hard to face.

To the south the operations in the Vosges served only to reinforce the lessons learnt in Champagne. The fighting here dragged on until the end of April. This time it was snow rather than rain which produced the climatic obstacle. Roads were even fewer than in the Champagne and mules became the only means of getting supplies up to the front line. This meant that the momentum of attack was sustained for an even shorter time. Once again the Germans showed their quick reactions in immediate counter-attacks against any position captured by the French. Not surprisingly, little ground was gained and the rugged terrain was ally to the defender. Hereafter this was to remain a quiet sector.

The British, meanwhile, had taken up Joffre's petulant invitation for a solo effort in the region of La Bassée. In comparison with the French attacks a very limited frontage had been chosen. The main reason was simply lack of artillery and, in particular, artillery ammunition. The point in the line chosen was the Neuve Chapelle salient, which had been captured by the Germans in October 1914. It masked the Aubers Ridge which dominated the British lines, and it was felt that once the ridge was captured German communications between La Bassée and Lille would be threatened.

43

Neuve Chapelle is significant because it was the first British attack against a trench system in the war and the methods used were to set the pattern for the next three years. The task was given over to Haig's First Army. The plan was to capture the village itself first, then fan out to secure the old British front line east of the village and finally capture the ridge itself. Preparations began in the last days of February. The attacking troops were withdrawn to the rear to carry out intensive rehearsals and detailed preparation orders were issued from Army HQ. Every aspect was considered at length, from the gradual placing in secrecy of the supporting artillery to practice in wire-cutting. Depots were set up behind the line with stores of engineer materials, small arms ammunition and grenades. For the first time in the war, the whole sector was photographed from the air and objective maps marking the lines of advance, which would be tied in with the artillery support, were issued. The staff work required for all this was intricate in the extreme, especially when it came to working out the artillery programme. The idea was that the guns would bombard an objective for a set length of time, by the end of which it was calculated that the attacking infantry would have almost reached it. It would then switch to the next objective and so on. By contrast to the French idea of a long softening up bombardment before the attack went in, only thirty-five minutes of fire were planned; in this way it was hoped to achieve surprise. Also, of course, the restricted ammunition supplies precluded any long bombardment.

On the night of the 9/10th March the attacking troops, fourteen battalions of them, filed into the trenches. Those they relieved had worked hard in preparation; gaps had been cut in the wire and ladders set up against the parapets of the front line trenches. The security arrangements had worked well and it was not until a few hours before the attack that the Germans in the opposite trenches became suspicious. The German trenches here were in any case weakly held and their second line of defence was ill prepared. The bombardment started at 0730 hrs on the 10th and thirty-five minutes later it lifted and the assaulting troops went in. In the centre the village of Neuve Chapelle had been captured and the old British line occupied within two hours. On the flanks things did not go so well. It was not until 1300 hrs that they were secured and the objectives reached. It was now that the weakness in communications showed itself. Telephone lines were cut by shell fire and runners failed to get through. Messages consequently took a long time to reach their destination and the fact that all of the initial objectives had been reached was not known for some hours at the higher headquarters. Consequently the attack on the ridge did not really get going before nightfall and the reserves had not by then been moved up.

The Germans therefore had time to bring up reinforcements and, even more important, improve their second line defences. They originally aimed to put in a counterattack on the 11th but, being unable to bring up sufficient reserves, had to postpone this for twenty-four hours. Haig ordered the attack to continue on the 11th, preceded by a bombardment, which was ineffective because a mist prevented observation. The German second line resisted all attempts to breach it and as the Official History said 'it was clear that until the new German position could be prepared for assault by an effective bombardment, the prospects of a successful advance by the infantry were negligible.' Haig wanted to continue the attack the next day, but the German counterattack came in first. In spite of the mist, which gave the Germans a covered approach to within fifty yards of the British line, the attack was held up, and orders were given for the British attack, originally scheduled for 1030 hrs, to go in. Again the mist and communication failures prevented progress and the disorganisation of the front line units caused Haig to call a halt to the battle.

Neuve Chapelle had had promising beginnings, but as with the French offensives to the south, it was the failure to react quickly to initial successes, thereby giving the enemy time to recover, which brought about eventual failure. There is no doubt, however, that the British had shown more promise than the French in their methods and the battle did much to restore French respect for the BEF. Unfortunately the main keys to success were not fully grasped. Sir Basil Liddell Hart names these as: 'the surprise attainable by a short bombardment that compensated for its brevity by its intensity'; and 'the sector being attacked must be sufficiently wide to prevent the defender's artillery commanding, or his reserves closing, the breach.' The offensives of the next two years would show what happened when the first point was ignored. The French, as a result of their own experiences, grasped the second point, but not the reasons behind it.

The problem of communications was tackled initially by burying the cables. At first it was done to a depth of only a few inches, but as the war progressed the cables were buried deeper and deeper. It became another ceaseless task for troops supposedly at rest. Another means of getting back information made its debut at Neuve Chapelle. Two flights of No. 3 Squadron Royal Flying Corps experimented with the flying of constant patrols above the battle, which reported its progress on landing. What were to become known as 'contact patrols' remained in the experimental stage throughout 1915, but the following year saw them acknowledged as a very vital part of any battle plan.

The fighting itself had taken on a pattern different from the attacks of 1914. Lieutenant Hobart of the Bengal Sappers and Miners (later Major-General and a famous armoured leader) has left us with a concise description of the fighting at Neuve Chapelle. Having received a call for engineer assistance from the 2nd Leicesters of the Indian Garhwal Brigade on the right flank, he went 'out along ditch. Found a pretty little hand grenade dog-fight going on. We couldn't get any further. Went up with subaltern to the end, leaving the men. Decided to build a barricade about 15 yards beyond the furthest point the Leicesters had been able to reach . . . Helped by Leicesters pulled sandbags out of German breastwork and passed on to men who built up the breastwork. The Germans got some men out into the ruins just behind and made things rather hot, as the parados was very low and we couldn't charge across as there was a morass in between. But they are rotten shots and didn't hit one of us.' Once one actually came to grips with the enemy the grenade was starting to become the ideal weapon. One bombed, shot and bayonetted one's way from traverse to traverse until one could go no further and then consolidated by putting up a barrier across the trench, drew breath and went on again. The importance of individual marksmanship, which had stood the British in such good stead in the opening battles, was on the wane. Machine-guns were coming into prominence and above all artillery was dominant. Small wonder then that in this type of fighting progress was slow and casualties heavy. The British at Neuve Chapelle suffered losses of 18,000 and advanced 1,000 yards on a 4,000 yard frontage, inflicting some 14,000 casualties on the Germans.

It was now the German turn to strike and see whether they would fare any better than the Allies. Ypres again was to be the target. Württemberg, who had failed to break through here in October, felt that the capture of Ypres would be beneficial for several reasons. By taking out the salient, his line would be shortened and hence he would have more troops to spare; it would mean the conquering of Belgium in entirety and would threaten the Allied flank; Ypres was a useful base for any projected Allied enterprise into Belgium. Finally it would provide a useful cover for the transfer of troops to the East for the projected Galician offensive. The Second Battle of Ypres was to be memorable for the introduction of a new weapon – gas. Funnily enough this was one of the few innovations which did not make its first appearance on the Western Front.

Rumours of the gas had been rife in the Allied press as early as September 1914, but it was not until the following month that the Germans produced a shell filled with an irritant, which they tried out in a local attack near Neuve Chapelle. Its effect was such that the Allies did not even notice its use and the fact was not discovered until after the war. As a result this design was scrapped and a Dr von Tappen, assisted by the illustrious Professor Haber, carried out experiments with xylyl bromide, a tear producing agent, which worked well in trials, again using an artillery shell. It was originally put in 15cm howitzer shells, but plans were also laid to put it into large mortar bombs and straightforward gas cylinders. It was felt that this would not so much knock troops out as merely incapacitate them long enough for their positions to be overrun. The German troops were provided with a simple mask, which could be doused with a protective chemical as required. The General Staff were finally persuaded to use it in their offensive against the Russians at Lodz in January 1915. A considerable number of gas shells were used against the Bolimow sector, but the results were not as expected. Instead of evaporating the extreme cold caused it to freeze, and thus it had no effect on the Russian troops.

Württemberg was now persuaded to try this gas. This time cylinders were to be used and by 8th April they were in position in the front line and the Germans were ready to attack. The disadvantage of using cylinders was that they were entirely dependant on a wind-from the right direction. It was not until the 22nd that the conditions were right. In the meantime the British captured some prisoners who spoke of these cylinders in the front line. Reports were sent back to Sir John French, but all the commanders from Brigade up to French himself, were sceptical and no preparations were made to combat it. According to the British Official History, no British officer believed that the Germans would resort to such an underhand trick. It should be noted that the Geneva Conventions of 1899 and 1907 had banned the use of poison gas; the Germans argued that xylyl was not poisonous.

The attack when it came on the 22nd was directed on the Pilckem Ridge to the north-east of Ypres. At this point the salient ran virtually east-west and was held by the French 87th Territorial, a survivor of First Ypres, and the 45th Algerian Divisions. Next door to them on the right flank was the Canadian Division, which had arrived at the front in its entirety in February. It was not until 1700 hrs that conditions were just right and the gas was released. The bulk of it fell on the Algerians and created instant panic. An eyewitness reported 'a panic-

The British 6-inch 26cwt Mark I howitzer. *Calibre:* 6 inches. *Barrel length:* 13.3 calibres. *Weight of gun and carriage:* 8,118lbs. *Elevation:* 0°-45°. *Traverse:* 8°. *Length:* 17 feet 6 inches. *Width:* 7 feet 10 inches. *Range:* 10,000 yards

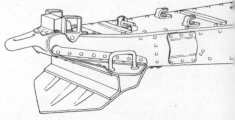

stricken rabble of Turcos and Zouaves with grey faces and protruding eyeballs, clutching their throats and choking as they ran, many of them dropping in their tracks and lying on the sodden earth with limbs convulsed and features distorted in death.' They took the Territorials with them in their panic and by nightfall a five mile gap had been opened up in the line, and the way to Ypres lay open. Luckily darkness saved the situation and the Germans, who had attacked with three divisions, contented themselves with consolidating the ground they had already won. The Canadians hastily

The French Schneider 155mm howitzer. *Weight of shell:* 95 lbs. *Range:* 10,500 yards with 1890 shell and 12,000 yards with 1915 shell. *Rate of fire:* 2 rounds per minute, but not more than 30 rounds per hour. *Traverse:* 3° left and right

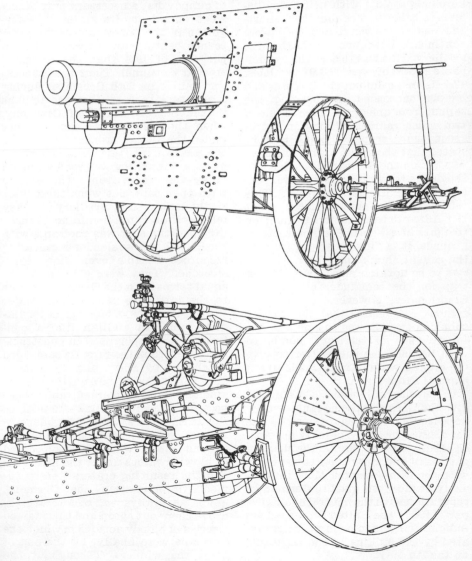

adjusted their positions through ninety degress so that they were facing north and the French, on Foch's orders, prepared to counterattack.

This was the start of a battle which was to continue until the end of May. Time and again the Germans would attack using the greenish-yellow clouds of gas as an overture. Using makeshift masks dunked in Sodium Bicarbonate and even, at times, handkerchiefs soaked with urine, the defenders held on. The munition shortage was at its worst and they were continually outgunned by the German artillery. This was to cost the participants a total of over 100,000 casualties. The Germans did not get to Ypres and merely succeeded in reducing the salient from one of six miles to one of two miles radius. Writing in retrospect the German Official History stated that the origin of this offensive was '. . . on the German side solely . . . the desire to try out the new weapon, gas, thoroughly at the front.' This reflects their pained surprise at the Allied determination to hold on to Ypres at all costs. Yet, on tactical grounds, it is difficult to justify why the salient should have been held. It was to be nothing more than a death trap for the remainder of the war. Emotionally, however, it became a symbol. The feeling that the invader should not be allowed to gain another square yard of territory, combined with British obstinacy never to give up ground voluntarily, made itself plain at First Ypres.

In the long run, the use of gas did not give the Germans the advantage they hoped for. The element of surprise was soon lost. The Allies quickly developed adequate protection in the shape of gasmasks and were soon to retaliate with the same weapon. More importantly, it did little good to Germany's reputation with the neutral countries, particularly the United States, where indignation was to be further aggravated by the sinking of the Lusitania on the 7th May.

One other new, or at least rediscovered tactic which was highlighted during this battle was tunnelling. The dogged fighting around Hill 60 at the south of the salient was notorious for its mining operations and so many men were killed underground that at the end of the war it was left as it was and still survives today, untouched save by nature. Mining had its origins in ancient warfare and was for centuries, especially after the invention of gunpowder, a necessary part of any siege operation. Its skills were forgotten in the latter part of the nineteenth century and it was not until the end of 1914 that the Germans started to tunnel. Their first success was gained on 20th December during a counterattack against the Indians in the neighbourhood of Givenchy, when they set off ten small mines under the Indian trenches, throwing the garrison into turmoil. Encouraged by this, tunnelling was soon going on along the whole front. The French tried open saps, but when these were easily destroyed by artillery fire they fell back on counter-mining tunnelling operations. It was the same with the British, whose slender engineering resources became even more overstretched. They were able to get on equal terms with the Germans thanks to the initiative of one man, Major Norton Griffiths, a Member of Parliament, and, in civilian life, a contractor who specialised in constructing underground sewers. He persuaded Kitchener to allow him to raise a special force of tunnellers from amongst his own men and these became the Tunnelling Companies Royal Engineers. Their first offensive success was at Hill 60 during the Second Ypres, when they succeeded in blowing mines under the hill itself and the resulting craters were occupied. Unfortunately the Germans, quick as always to counterattack, drove them out again and this started a series of bloody actions in which the Germans were finally, by the end of May, the winners. Throughout the

remainder of the year the Germans were to have the ascendancy in the war underground, but the next year would put the Allies on equal terms.

The postponed offensive in Artois was the next Allied blow. It will be remembered that Joffre's condition to Sir John French for launching this attack was that he should be allowed to have his two corps north of Ypres available for this operation. This was finally reluctantly agreed by French at the Chantilly Conference of 29th March. The date of the attack was fixed for 1st May and the British were to launch another subsidiary attack in the Aubers Ridge area. The actual scene of the French attack was to be the Vimy Ridge north of Arras, which dominated the ground to east and west. A small portion of one of the spurs, Notre Dame de Lorette, was in French hands already, a trophy of the December operations, and it was planned to launch a preparatory attack from here, as well as another

Aubers Ridge, May 1915. British reinforcements pass through a mine crater which shelters the wounded of both sides

subsidiary attack towards the River Scarpe. It was hoped that this, along with the British attack, would keep the German reserves away from Vimy Ridge.

Foch's appreciation of the situation, together with his deductions from the earlier offensives, left him with the conclusion that success was dependent on overwhelming superiority of men and artillery. The Tenth Army, which was to carry out the attack, was allotted no less than eighteen divisions, together with three cavalry divisions, which would exploit the breakthrough; this was against only four German divisions. Foch was given 1,252 guns, of which 293 were heavy. He abandoned the element of surprise and instead plumped for a four day bombardment, 'slow, methodical, and

49

prolonged, with the object of destroying the enemy's morale, disorganising his defensive measures and breaking up his obstacles and strongpoints.' The actual assault was to be preceded by a comparatively short bombardment of four hours length. The attack was to be broken down into a series of short limited objectives, the first day's being the three mile stage to the crest of the ridge. Yet Foch laid down at the same time that by far the greatest part of Tenth Army must be committed to the initial attack; in fact only 30 out of 225 battalions were left as reserve to the army commander, General d'Urbal. Later, two divisions, together with the cavalry, were earmarked as an additional reserve, but were placed even further behind the line. Unfortunately d'Urbal in his efforts to bolster up his reserve also withdrew the few uncommitted reserves of the corps actually engaged. Thus it was obvious that the same recurrent problem of lack of immediate reserves to reinforce success was bound to crop up. Too much reliance, as well, was being placed on the attacking troops having the stamina to continue the attack until what reserves there were could be deployed to pass through them.

Again detailed preparation, in which Neuve Chapelle had set the tone, was the order of the day. Pétain's XXXIII Corps on the left centre was particularly methodical, with Pétain himself checking the registration of each single gun. All the innovations of Neuve Chapelle in the way of preparation were used, together with some new ones such as the digging of attack trenches 100 yards forward of the front line and the widening of communication trenches to take two way traffic. The Germans appeared to remain blissfully unaware of what was going on, but considering the natural strength of the position together with the German defences, two solid heavily fortified trench lines, increasing to as much as five or six in places, the Germans may have

felt no need to make special preparations.

The date for the opening of operations was postponed until 4th May when the bombardment started and bad weather on the 7th caused d'Urbal to prolong it for two extra days. General Sir Henry Wilson, chief British liaison officer at Joffre's headquarters, witnessed the opening of the attack on the 9th. 'The Frenchmen began to fire at 0600 hours and fired till 1000 hours . . . No living person has ever before heard or seen such a thing. The shells passing over my head made one steady hiss. At 1000 hours, to the second, the guns stopped and the whole long line of French infantry, as far as I could see to the north and south, rose up out of their trenches and went forward. The next moment the guns opened again with a barrage. A most wonderful sight. I watched the infantry take all the trenches within sight with few losses, and then, at 1100 hours, I came away.' Wilson had been watching Pétain's Corps and their meticulous preparations appeared to have paid off, for by 1130 hours they were on the summit of the ridge, albeit with heavy casualties. 'The plain of Douai comes into sight with its factories and countless red-roofed cottages – the great city we are going to reconquer. Wild and uncontrollable, the enormous wave sweeps forward. Impossible to check the men, not even for a moment to dress the ranks. Everyone is running – how can anyone not run at the sight of the Boches below streaming back towards Carleul and Souchez? It is victory! It is breakthrough!' Unfortunately the flanking formations were not so successful and only XX Corps on Pétain's immediate right made anything approaching his progress. At the same time the joint bugbears of poor communications and lack of immediate reserves came into play. The Germans were able to put in a couple of fresh divisions, just below the crest, thus obscured from Pétain's troops, and a series of counterattacks slowly wore

50

away the French gains. By 15th May thirteen German divisions were facing the Tenth Army and the chance of victory had gone. There was now a pause and it was not until a month later that a final desperate effort was made to take the ridge. It had in the meantime been heavily reinforced in artillery, fortifications and men and the attackers stood little chance. On the 18th Foch finally realised that further effort was useless.

The subsidiary attacks had also come to nothing. The French had made use of five mines, much in the German style, but, after initial success, had failed against immediate German counterattack. The British attack on Aubers Ridge had retained the idea of the short bombardment, forty minutes this time. However it was the shortage of artillery ammunition (only twenty per cent of French's laid down monthly requirement was manufactured in April and some of this had been needed up at Ypres), rather than the desire for surprise which dictated this. The German defences had been much improved since Neuve Chapelle, concrete emplacements, deeper dugouts and thicker wire, and the short bombardment failed even to cut the wire and merely alerted the defenders. The British suffered 12,000 casualties, mainly victims to subtly located machine-guns, in less than twenty-four hours, and Haig called off the attack.

The British, however, still felt morally bound to give the French Tenth Army some support and so they planned another attack. First of all though they took over another 5,500 yards of front, south of the La Bassée Canal, from the French. Two divisions, the 2nd and 7th, were selected for the new attack which was to take place on a limited front and envisaged an advance of no more than 1,000 yards to take place at Festubert. Haig, in view of the failure at Aubers Ridge, felt that 'it was necessary now to proceed methodically and break down the enemy's strongpoints and entrenchments. An accurate and so fairly long bombardment will be necessary.' The artillery fire plan was much more detailed than before. Instead of a straightforward bombardment of the enemy's defences each battery was given a specific task, either wirecutting, counter-battery work, parapet destruction or harassing fire. However a plan of this sort needs a senior artillery officer to coordinate it and this Haig did not have. There was also the problem, which had been in existence for some time, of faulty ammunition. Shoddy manufacture had led to many complaints of shells bursting prematurely or landing short within the British lines, or sometimes not even exploding on impact. The lack of coordination and poor quality ammunition seriously detracted from what, in theory, was a sound plan.

However, Festubert is notable as the first example of a set piece night attack made by the British during the war. The attack went in just before midnight on 15th May and in the centre the Germans were taken by surprise and their lines penetrated. However on the flanks little success was to be had as the enemy was alert. Once again the German defence system, speedy counterattacks and the dwindling stocks of artillery ammunition brought the battle to a halt and by the 26th it was all over. The British had lost another 16,000 men for minimal gains.

By the end of May the Allies had been repulsed everywhere along the front. The Germans had been able to do as they wished in transferring troops to the east. Their offensive against the Russians was launched on 2nd May and by the beginning of August, along with the Austrians, they had rolled the Russians back three hundred miles and inflicted approaching two million casualties. If the Russians were to hold on at all something else must be done in the west to relieve the pressure.

Possible solutions

The deductions made by the Allies as a result of their attempts on the German front in the Spring and early Summer of 1915 had convinced them that the key to success lay in quantity. The larger the number of men and guns that there were available the greater the chances of a breakthrough. It was the principle of the sledgehammer; the greater the weight of metal that could be flung at the German defences the more likely they were to crumble. Since there was a limit to the number of guns one could employ the maximum weight of metal could only be produced by a prolonged bombardment. Yet there were dangerous fallacies in this argument. The Germans had realised that the best way to counter a heavy bombardment was to construct more solid defences with deeper shelters to protect their troops. This had already become apparent on Vimy Ridge. The element of surprise had also been lost and the Germans had had time to muster their reserves in good time,

their ability to launch immediate counterattacks before the attackers had had time to consolidate their gains proving highly successful. By their use of gas they had shown that there was another possible answer to the problem.

The main problem that faced the Allies in attack was the use of reserves. They had come to realise that to attempt a breakthrough on a narrow front would lead only to disaster. Yet to attack on a wide front meant that the reserves were going to be stretched, that is if the basic principle of attack en masse, which committed troops to go into the attack shoulder to shoulder, was to be followed. This was the French theory and their experiences up until now had not dissuaded them from the belief that a mass concentration of bayonets at the decisive point led to victory. In order, therefore, to make the best use of reserves (and it was realised that they were essential) they must be concentrated rather than dispersed along the whole front so that they could be used to reinforce success and not be frittered away. To allow them to be brought up in time the principle of limited objectives was introduced. However, although this gave more chance of securing what had already been captured, it gave the enemy more time to reorganise and went against that fundamental principle of attack of maintaining momentum. But even where success was achieved the reserves had never been brought up quickly enough and the reason for this, more than anything else, was the 'fog of war'. Primitive communications and the extreme difficulty of being able to observe what was happening once the enemy's front line had been entered meant that headquarters in the rear were left for long periods in the dark as to the true situation. There was, consequently, a natural tendency to wait for a clear picture to emerge before taking decisions, which would be impossible to reverse once they had been put into effect. This then was the dilemma which faced the Allies in the mid summer of 1915.

As early as May Joffre was planning for a gigantic autumn offensive, which would finally achieve total victory. Yet a number of his commanders were becoming disillusioned with this idea of remaining permanently on the offensive. The 100,000 casualties of the early months of 1915 had dampened their ardour. In particular the politicians led by Clemenceau attacked Joffre before the Parliamentary Army Committee, arguing that 'if things go on as they are, there will be a revolt of the generals against the High Command.' President Poincaré, visiting the front in early July, was approached by all six of the corps commanders who had taken part in

Joffre with President Poincaré. When the latter visited the front in July 1915 he heard a barrage of complaints against Joffre's policy of remaining permanently on the offensive

Troops of the Royal Naval Division go over the top in Gallipoli which, far from producing the decisive blow, soon degenerated into another trench deadlock à la Western Front

the Arras attacks. 'Pray, Monsieur le President, do what you can to put a stop to these local offensives; the instrument of victory is being broken in our hands,' as IX Corps commander put it. Pétain felt that the fault lay in 'starting an offensive without sufficiently consulting those who have to carry it out'. If the morale of the corps commanders was low that of the front line troops was even lower. Foch, too, who had up until now been Joffre's most ardent disciple, was beginning to realise that the chances of an early triumphant end to the war were slim.

Joffre was not to be thwarted and having made some minor concessions – eight days leave for the troops and the promise of greater delegation to subordinates, continued to plan. The politicians on both sides of the Chan-

nel had not been enthusiastic for another reason. The Allies had landed at Gallipoli on 23rd April and the Easterners were full of hope that this would produce the decisive blow, which had been lacking in the West. It was, however, to be a campaign of missed opportunities and settled into a trench-bound deadlock like the Western Front. It certainly did nothing to ease the pressure on the Russians. And so the politicians very reluctantly allowed Joffre to press ahead with his preparations.

Once again the huge German salient bound by Arras in the north and Champagne in the south hypnotised Joffre. Again he saw the operation as being one of simultaneous effort in Champagne and Artois and again he requested British assistance in the northern offensive. Kitchener's New Armies of civilian volunteers were now in the process of being shipped to France and Joffre cast envious glances at them. With characteristic bluntness he presented his plan to Sir John

French on 4th June, demanding at the same time that the British should take over an additional twenty miles of front south of Arras in order to relieve Pétain's Second Army for the attack, and also that the British should put in an attack either north or south of the French effort at Vimy. Sir John acted on the first by creating a new Third Army which took over the line from the River Somme to Hebuterne fifteen miles to the north. He was not prepared to take over the extra five miles or so south of the river. He also agreed to strike between Lens and La Bassée. Haig, whose army was detailed for the attack, was unhappy, not merely with the site chosen which was a built-up area which would restrict movement, but also with the idea of an attack. The supplies of guns and shells were still woefully inadequate and he felt that it would be better to be content with active defence as opposed to frittering the slender stocks of ammunition on what appeared to be merely a subsid-

iary attack in support of the French. At first Sir John would not wear this argument, but he came round to Haig's point of view in time for a joint conference at Foch's headquarters on 27th July. However, Foch overruled him and the plans for the Lens attack went ahead.

In essence Joffre's scheme allocated the majority of the troops available to Castelnau, who was to command the Champagne offensive. Twenty-seven divisions were given to Pétain for the major attack on an eighteen mile front east of Reims and further seven to de Langle de Cary for a subsidiary effort west of Reims. By contrast only seventeen divisions were available to Foch at Arras, attacking on a twelve mile front. The reason given was that the ground was more favourable in Champagne. Joffre had refused to acknowledge this argument when used by the British objecting to the location for their attack. The British planned to attack on a six mile front with six divisions with Sir John

Crown Prince Rupprecht of Bavaria, commander of the German Sixth Army

French retaining a further three in reserve under his own control. This was in contrast to the French, who resolved this time to place their reserves close up behind the attacking troops. As regards artillery, Joffre, by stripping fortresses and quieter parts of the line, managed to raise 850 guns for Pétain and 420 for Foch. The British, on the other hand, only had a mere 114 and Haig hoped to offset this disparity by playing the Germans at their own game in the use of gas. The date of attack was originally fixed as 7th September, but in order to allow more time for careful preparation was put back until the 27th.

In August the Germans in Artois and Champagne got wind of the preparations for the attack. Their requests for reinforcements fell on deaf ears when they reached Falkenhayn and caused Einem in Champagne and Prince Rupprecht in the north to wonder whether their deductions were correct after all. Certainly Einem was quite happy on 21st September, as the French bombardment started, to return to Germany for a visit to the Kaiser's headquarters. However, every

fresh attempt at an attack by the Allies had taught the Germans something new about the art of defence and their methods had altered radically since the beginning of the year. Gone was the idea of the single line bolstered by machine-gun posts to the rear. Instead Falkenhayn had laid down that an additional defence line should be constructed to the rear of the machine-guns, if possible on a reverse slope so that it would be unobserved. These would be occupied by the reserve battalions of the regiments in line, whose forward battalions would, if need be, fall back on the second line under artillery cover. The artillery had been trained in three separate defensive techniques: bombardment of the enemy's forming up places *(Zerstörungsfeuer)*, sharp fire on the enemy front line at the moment of attack *(Vernichtungsfeuer)* and once the attack had been launched a covering barrage for their own front line *(Sperrfeuer)*. Nevertheless, in spite of these new methods, the Germans were thin on the ground – six divisions against seventeen in Artois and seven against the twenty-seven French east of Reims. What is more, there were virtually no reserves, only about seven divisions and some cavalry to cover both fronts.

The Allied bombardment began on the 21st and once again the German lines were subject to concentrated pulverisation. Even the British effort sounded impressive to those present, although as one wrote, 'we thought a lot of the bombardment at the time, but it was nothing to what we were used to in later years'. Haig appreciated only too well how dependent the gas was on wind and had agreed with Foch that the attack would be reduced to only two divisions if the wind were not favourable. Meanwhile Joffre issued a special order of the day telling the attacking troops that *'votre élan sera irrésistible'*.

The first to attack on the 25th were the British, who went over the top at 0630 hours. Before this there had been

Falkenhayn

a tense scene at Haig's headquarters when his meteorological officer had been summoned at 0300 hours and had expressed the opinion that the wind would soon veer from south-east to south. At 0500 hours Haig stood outside and asked his senior aide-de-camp, Lieutenant-Colonel Fletcher, to light a cigarette. The smoke from it drifted gently towards the north-east, not the most favourable direction, but it was too late to change the orders and at 0550 hours the cylinders were unscrewed. 'The gas was already rising into the air and forming into a rolling grey cloud. Showers of small chalk fell among the waiting men. The top layer of hessian bags on the parapet was breaking, lifting ragged ears to the dull sky. Through the rolling thunder of the bombardment could be heard a shearing-of-glass noise as the air above the trench was torn across by machine-gun bullets. Distant rockets soared and broke into colours; down fell the German shells. The waiting men crouched.' This was how the author Henry Williamson, himself a temporary gas officer with 1st Division, saw the

start of the battle. This division was on the left and suffered both from the wind, which blew the gas back into their trenches, and from the fact that the forty minutes lapse gave the Germans time to make ready. The leading two battalions of 19th Brigade lost some 800 men and the attack was a washout from the start.

In the centre however it was a different story. 15th Scottish Division, representing the New Armies, with the wind blowing in the right direction, stormed through the German trenches and by the end of the day was clinging on to Hill 70, a penetration of some two miles. On its right the 47th London Division (Territorial) managed to capture the village of Loos. It was now that tragedy struck. Haig urgently needed his reserves to exploit his successes and Sir John French insisted that these, in the shape of the newly formed XI Corps, should remain under his personal control. The three reserve divisions were New Army formations and two of them, the 21st and 24th Divisions, had been marching up to the front over the past three nights, moving by night to avoid detection by enemy aircraft. On the night of 24th September they were still twenty miles away. Progress that night became slower and slower and they still had over five miles to go when they were halted at dawn on the 25th. It was not until midday that Sir John finally agreed that Haig could have them and by then it was too late. They were in no position to attack until next day and when they did, tired and bewildered, they were massacred by the German machine gunners, who had had time to reorganise. Once again the chance had been lost and although the attacks were continued until 4th November in response to requests by Joffre, no further gains were made. French's handling of the reserves cost him his command and by the end of the year Haig had taken over as commander of the British armies in France.

To the right of the British the French Tenth Army started its attacks at 1245 hours on the 25th. In spite of careful preparation the German defence proved too much for the French. Only on the left was there any progress and attempts to exploit this on the 26th came to virtually nothing and as a result Foch was ordered by Joffre to 'stop the attacks of the Tenth Army, taking care to avoid giving the British the impression that we are leaving them to attack alone, or the Germans that our offensive is slackening off. Economise ammunition.' The main reason for this was that Joffre was now devoting his attention to the Champagne where the early results had shown more promise. The Germans had concentrated most of their effort in the second line of defence and consequently Castelnau succeeded on the first day in breaking through ten miles of the German first line, albeit with heavy casualties. The second line was reached on the next day along a seven mile frontage but only one small lodgement was made. Three more desperate days of fighting followed but again with no result. Yet at the end of the first day the French had been confident enough to bring forward no less than eight cavalry divisions with orders to make 'a relentless pursuit without waiting for the infantry.' The following weeks brought renewed efforts on all three sectors; Foch in particular was determined to wrest Vimy Ridge from the Germans before winter finally set in. Finally Joffre was forced to call a halt. Gains in terms of ground had been few and the Allies suffered 250,000 casualties as against 140,000 German.

Once again winter had arrived and on both sides of the line staffs and fighting troops alike were thankful to retire to their respective corners and lick their wounds. As far as the Allies were concerned, the 1915 campaign had not produced, as had been confidently expected, the key that would unlock the door to success. Several lessons had been learnt, but it was very questionable as to whether they were the right ones. They are best summed up in Foch's report on the past operations, submitted on 10th November 1915. He began by baldly stating that the campaign of 1915 had failed simply through lack of artillery ammunition. With the casualty figures for the autumn attacks fresh in his mind, he then went on to say 'in our attacks across ground fortified in depth we must above all spare our infantry, in order that it may last through the time inevitably necessary for the battle to be completed.' In order to do this there must be proper preparation and by this Foch meant artillery fire. 'It is a fact that the infantry attack always halts and fails at that point where the preparation has not been sufficient'. As to the method of attack, 'the succession of obstacles which an offensive encounters in its advance leads inevitably to a succession of attacks . . . a series of efforts following each other as closely as possible. We must give up the idea of an assault undertaken with more or less deep and dense masses, with the reserves following closely on the heels of the first line, and with the idea of carrying at a single bound a whole series of obstacles. This method has never succeeded.' He summed his ideas up in a further memorandum dated 6th December. 'The offensive draws its strength (1) from its power of destruction [artillery, gas] . . . (2) from its ability to renew promptly its successive action against each succeeding line. Destruction, repetition; these are its essential characteristics. The one sought for and therefore to be reinforced; the other forced upon us and therefore to be abridged.'

In other words Foch foresaw an attack as consisting of a long and heavy preparatory bombardment followed by an assault on limited objectives, reconsolidation, further bombardment, further assaults and so on until the breach was finally made. Unfortunately, this doctrine played right into the hands of the Germans, whose methods of defence, as we have seen, worked best against the theory of limited objectives. The whole element of surprise had been cast into the wastepaper basket and, as that eminent military historian, Major-General J F C Fuller, put it, 'tactics were reduced to a matter of push of pikes – actually push of shells – drill took the place of manoeuvre, method of surprise, and bombardments replaced leadership.'

Yet the search for new weapons in order to achieve surprise was not utterly abandoned. We have already seen the German contributions of gas and underground mining; they introduced yet another tactic in 1915. As early as 1900, the Germans had developed a flamethrower and in 1911 three Pioneer Battalions had been issued with it. According to the French Official History the first flame attack took place at Malancourt Wood between the Argonne and the Meuse in October 1914. The next attack was also against the French near Verdun in February 1915, but it was not until July that this weapon was used to any great extent and this time the British were the victims. The scene of the attack was the grounds of the ruined Hooge Château, which had seen so much fighting in the battles for Ypres. To the north the Germans held a salient with its base upon Bellewaarde Lake and in order to straighten the line wanted to clear the British from the Château. The opposing trenches were perilously close here, being as little as fifteen yards apart at one point. At 0315 hours on 30th July the Germans sprayed liquid fire from six flamethrowers into the British trenches, held by the 8th Rifle Brigade. A survivor described the effect as '. . . a sudden hissing sound, and a bright crimson glare over the crater turned the whole scene red. As I looked I saw three of four distinct jets of flame, like a line of powerful fire hoses spraying fire instead of water, shoot across my fire trench. How long this lasted is impossible to say, probably not more than a minute, but the effect was so stupefying that I was utterly unable for some moments to think correctly. About a dozen men of Number 2 Platoon were all that I could find. Those who faced the flame attack were never seen again.' Complete surprise was achieved and the liquid fire was speedily followed up by a furious German bayonet attack and all objectives were taken. Efforts to counterattack the same afternoon failed dismally against German machine-gun supremacy and the Germans were able to hold on to their gains. The flamethrower was very bulky and could only be used successfully where the trenches were fairly close, not more than twenty-five yards apart. There were not many places along the line where this was so, but all the same the Germans were to use it frequently when they took to the attack.

As early as October 1914 imaginative minds on the British side had been considering new methods of dealing with entrenched positions in the attack. The invention of the tank cannot be attributed to any one man. In the beginning it was a number of separate agencies all tackling the same problem and finally all coming up with much the same answer. As far as can be established the original germ was sown in a discussion between Colonel Hankey of the Committee for Imperial Defence, Colonel Swinton, the official war correspondent at the front, and Captain Tulloch, an artilleryman and gunnery expert, on 21st October. Both politicians and soldiers were sounded out and Hankey followed this up in his Boxing Day Memo when considering special devices; he wrote: 'Numbers of large heavy rollers, themselves bullet proof, propelled from behind by motor engines, geared very low, the driving wheels fitted with "caterpillar" driving gear to grip the ground, the driver's seat armoured and with a Maxim gun fitted. The object of this device would be to roll down the barbed wire by sheer weight, to give some cover to men creeping up behind, and to support the advance with machine-gun fire . . .' At the same time the Admiralty, which had been employing armoured cars in Flanders and elsewhere since the beginning of the war, was working on similar lines. Suggestions were put by members of the Royal Naval Air Service to their chief in the Admiralty, Commodore Sueter, who passed them on to the First Lord, Winston Churchill, who thought of some ideas himself. They varied from armoured shields on wheels for the protection of infantry to the idea of a 'landship' of 300 tons weight mounting three twin 4-inch naval guns. Churchill saw Hankey's Boxing Day Memo and in a letter to Asquith dated 5th January suggested that 'it would be quite easy in a short time to fit up a number of steam tractors with small armoured shelters, in which men and machine-guns could be placed, which would be bullet-proof . . . The caterpillar system would enable trenches to be crossed quite easily, and the weight of the machine would destroy all wire entanglements.' In February Churchill formed a Landships Committee, and after pursuing various red herrings, the committee in June decided on a machine with the following specifications – speed of not less than 4mph on level ground, capable of sharp turns at top speed, reversing capability, ability to climb a 5 foot earth parapet with a 1-in-1 slope, gap crossing ability of 8 feet, radius of action of 20 miles and a crew of ten with two machine-guns and one QF gun.

The caterpillar system as used on the American Holt Tractor was selected as the means to achieve the necessary mobility and production of a prototype went ahead at the firm of Foster's of Lincoln. However it soon became apparent that this first model or 'Little Willie' as it became called, was topheavy and unlikely to be able to cross the eight foot gap and a rhomboidal design was speedily developed in its place. The wooden mock-

up of 'Big Willie' was first shown in September and at the end of the year a Major Hugh Elles was sent back from GHQ in France to report on it. The results were favourable and Haig put in for an initial order of forty. At the same time the French started to try to find a solution on the same lines and a Colonel Estienne was ordered to carry out experiments in conjunction with the Schneider-Creusot factory. In the British case it was to be some months before these machines appeared on the battlefield and the French, being a good six months behind, were to take even longer. These, however, were the first tentative steps by the Allies to ensure that the element of surprise was not entirely ignored on the battlefield.

The troglodyte existence of the winter of 1915–16 became much more regulated than that of the previous winter. The reasons, as explained by the Medical Officer of the 2nd Royal Welsh Fusiliers in his diary, were that 'the line was stable. The antagonists were marking time. The large civil population that the war had brought into the field partly trained had to be inured to campaigning. There was the experience and, soon, the material that were lacking in 1914—15. The trench system was a year old: much labour was needed to repair and re-make trenches that collapsed with time and weather as well as damage by shell-fire. New trenches and keeps were made. There was an unlimited supply of sand-bags for revetting . . . Hundreds of miles of duckboard were laid to mitigate the mud and the consequent wastage by trench-foot.' The trenches were undoubtedly more comfortable, although the British lagged behind the Germans and French. 'The French army was more ingenious than ours at supplying home comforts. Their trench shelters were hollowed out under banks and lined with

By late 1915 the trenches were comparatively sophisticated. These *poilus* have a wooden dugout entrance

60

hurdles cut from the hedges, which they also used to revet the sides of their trenches so that the earth would not cave in. These shelters were cosy rather than secure, which did not so much matter since the French intended to go forward in the spring . . .' The Germans on the other hand were now going in for deep dugouts, as Charles Carrington goes on to describe: 'The standard pattern was a length of plank-lined tunnel under the parapet, ten feet or more below ground level, to which you descended by a steep flight of fifteen or twenty cellar steps. Every mine dugout had at least two such entrances and in the Leipzig Redoubt near Thiepval I have seen dugouts connected underground, with eight or nine narrow stairways up to different fire-bays.' The British relied on sandbags and Carrington lays claim that 'the art of filling and laying sandbags – bonded like brickwork, sloped at the most effective angle, and hammered flat with a spade – was a British trench accomplishment.'

Trench weapons, too, were not the homemade affairs of the year before. The Germans remained ahead of the Allies in this field during 1915, but there were noticeable improvements. The grenade was properly manufactured and had become one of the most important parts of the trench armoury. It was no longer always thrown by hand. Other methods such as the bomb thrower, which worked on the principle of the Roman catapult, and the rifle grenade were introduced. The Allies produced proper trench mortars and the British Stokes Mortar, which could fire bombs as fast as they could be loaded, became the forerunner of the modern infantry mortar. The Very pistol which fired white or coloured flares made its appearance this year. The British also introduced a light machine gun in the shape of the Lewis Gun, so called after its inventor Colonel Lewis of the United

A metal shield for a German machine gun

States army. Compared with the Vickers Machine Gun, with its weight of 68 lbs, the Lewis Gun only weighed 28 lbs and was therefore more manoeuvreable in the narrow confines of the trenches. It gradually started to replace the Vickers, which were concentrated into companies of sixteen guns under the direct control of brigade headquarters. All these new weapons required much special training and a large proportion of men of any battalion started to find themselves being sent on courses at schools behind the line to learn to handle them. An official British pamphlet, 'Notes for Officers on Trench Warfare' dated March 1916, makes the plea that in spite of this specialisation every man must be trained to be an infantryman first. This might seem rather ludicrous, but the training of the New Army formations was by no means complete by the time they reached the front. It was not uncommon for a soldier never to have fired his rifle, such was the shortage of equipment and training areas at home.

Much had happened in the realm of communications. Cable did not seem to have provided the complete answer as, even when buried, it was still vulnerable to shellfire. The French, in preparation for their offensives from the early summer onwards, laid duplicate and even triplicate line systems but communications with the front line still broke down. Alternative means had to be found. Signalling lamps were one answer, but these had the inherent disadvantage of being able to send messages only one way, to the rear, as otherwise they would be intercepted by the enemy. Both sides also started to use pigeons, which had been used by the Intelligence branches at the beginning of the war.

Another possibility was wireless. We have seen how the British were working on a lighter set for use in aircraft and it was these lighter sets which were tried on the ground. As early as June 1915 the British V Corps were experimenting with four of these

German battle order, late 1915. The gas mask and the stick bomb have come to the fore as essential equipment

sets working from a battalion through two brigades to a division and finally to a lorry-borne set at corps head-quarters. The results were not a total failure, but these sets were too un-wieldy to be carried about the trenches and their aerials were a tempting target for enemy artillery and trench mortars. The Germans had also developed jamming sets to interrupt air-ground artillery communications.

They did the same with line and Allied suspicions were aroused when trench raids and reliefs seemed to bring down accurate artillery fire time and again. On the French front they physically tapped the lines and the noticeable cross talk on all British forward lines indicated that messages were being transmitted via the earths through the ground. The answer was to run the earths back and by the beginning of 1916 these were running back as far as a thousand yards from the telephone set. The Germans were helped in their interceptions by the fact that there

was little attempt at security on the telephone.

While the French were content to let their front line troops rest (and whenever possible this meant manning the front line with second line troops), the British renewed their battle to dominate No Man's Land. Raiding really came into its own during this winter and the tone was quickly set with a series of successful raids by the Canadians astride the River Douve in November 1915. The Germans were content to follow a policy of 'live and let live', when permitted, but in the more active sectors of the line were quick to retaliate in kind, although, like the French, they found it simpler to try to dominate No Man's Land by fire. British orders made it quite clear that 'the forthcoming winter months are to be utilised not for passive defence but for exhausting the enemy's troops and for training all branches in future operations.'

Christmas 1915 passed, without the fraternisation of the year before, and the commanders of both sides began scheming up ways of obtaining victory in the west in 1916.

Verdun and the Somme

The outline strategy for 1916 had been agreed at a conference of the Allied commanders at Chantilly at the beginning of December 1915. The plan was for a simultaneous assault on three fronts, Italian, Russian and Western. March was originally envisaged as the time for attack, but it soon became apparent that this was too early. Nobody, except the French, expected to be adequately equipped for an offensive until at least May and so Joffre put the date back until 1st July. The conference was also a victory for the westerners in that it laid down that, as far as the Western Allies were concerned, every available division should be retained in France. Gallipoli was to be evacuated. There was also a strong lobby for the evacuation of Salonika, but it did not prevail and the Franco-British force of eight divisions stayed.

Joffre's plan for the west envisaged a joint Anglo-French attack astride the Somme from Lassigny to Arras, a front of sixty miles. He had finally given up his theme song of 1915, namely the breaking of the great German salient with simultaneous blows at both sides of its neck, and was now going for a frontal punch. He asked Foch to study a potential offensive south of the Somme, while requesting Haig's views on a British attack north of the river. In a letter to Haig in January, just after suggesting to him in person that the British should carry out a large-scale attack in April, Joffre said 'I regard it as indispensable that before the general offensive, the British army should seek to wear down the German forces by wide and powerful offensives, as the French did in 1915.' This produced a difference of opinion. Haig could well understand why the French were not willing to expend manpower on this type of preliminary attack. In a letter to Kitchener dated 19th January he said: 'The fact is the French "dépôts" are so

Crown Prince Wilhelm, commander of the German Fifth Army which spearheaded the onslaught against Verdun

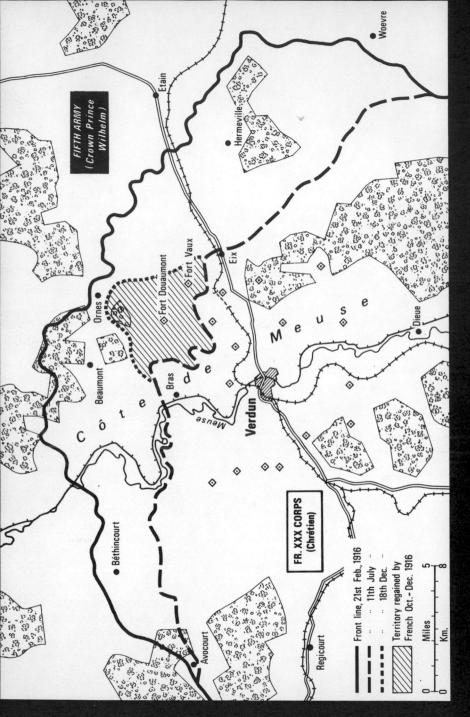

The battle for Verdun, February/December 1916

empty of troops that their army is only capable of one big effort in their opinion.' He was equally loath to see British troops used up in this way. In a strongly worded letter to Joffre on 1st February he argued that the carrying out of 'wearing-down' attacks in April and May would have little effect on the Germans because they would have plenty of time to make good their losses in time for the main attack. It would mean losses for little gain and public opinion in both Britain and France would not wear this. Haig did not tell Joffre, but another reason for his doubts was that he was very worried about the state of training of the New Army divisions and felt that it would take him six months to get them up to the necessary standard. A fortnight later the two men reached a compromise. Haig agreed to put in a preparatory attack at Armentières just before the main attack went in and also agreed to relieve the Tenth French Army, which had been sandwiched by the British at Arras since August. In return, Joffre dropped his proposals for attacks in April and May. Interestingly, Foch was not in favour of Joffre's plan, believing that the sector south of the Somme was a strategic dead-end, being bounded by the 'ditch' of the Somme. If he had had his way another attempt would have been made at Vimy Ridge, which he was convinced was the key to the whole German line. As it was, he did manage to get one modification made to the plan in that it was agreed that one French corps would attack north of the Somme. Liddell Hart commented on this, 'this change fulfilled the military theory that the forces operating on either side of such a dividing barrier should be under one command, to ensure co-ordination. But it was to prove a case where theory had practical drawbacks, for in the outcome the presence of a French corps north of the river complicated the arrangements for synchronised action, and cramped the free action of the British right wing.'

But this is to anticipate. Before the Allies had a chance to get down to detailed planning they were forestalled by the German initiative at Verdun in February.

The dilemma which the Central Powers found themselves in, when considering their overall plan for 1916, was basically that of whether to remain on the defensive or to attack. After failures of the Allied attacks in the west defence was a tempting proposition to the Germans, but it would mean firstly that the war might drag on for years and secondly that the Russians might break through on the Austro-Hungarian front, where morale was steadily dropping. If an attack was to be mounted, the question was where? It was very tempting to follow up the successes against the Russians, but in the vastness of that country invading armies would be swallowed up. The Balkans and the Italian front could only be considered as minor theatres. And so the Western Front was left. To Falkenhayn, Germany's most dangerous enemy was Britain: 'Germany can expect no mercy from this enemy, so long as he retains the slightest hope of achieving his object.' Britain could be crippled by unrestricted submarine warfare, but this might well turn the neutral countries against Germany and even worse bring the USA into the war on the Allied side. If an attack was made against the British army it still left the French to be dealt with. Falkenhayn, in his appreciation of the situation, was thus left with one solution, an attack against the French. He justified it by saying '. . . the strain on France has almost reached breaking point – though it is certainly borne with the most remarkable devotion. It we succeeded in opening the eyes of of her people to the fact that in a military sense they have nothing more to hope for, that breaking point would be reached and England's best sword would be knocked out of her hand . . . We can probably do enough for our purposes with limited resources. Within our reach behind the French sector of the Western Front there are objectives for the retention of which the French General Staff would be compelled to throw in every man they have. If they do the forces of France will bleed to death – as there can be no question of a voluntary withdrawal – whether we reach our goal or not.'

Falkenhayn was going for nothing less than the wholesale massacre of the French army and his belief that the French would be prepared to allow this to happen in order to defend certain parts of their line showed an incisive understanding of his opponent. To be sure of confronting the French, as opposed to the British, the attack would have to be south of the Somme. Only two areas would really arouse French emotions, Verdun and Belfort, two of the ancient fortresses of France. The French attempts in the Vosges in the winter of 1914–15 had shown how difficult it was to attack at Belfort and hence Falkenhayn selected Verdun – 'Verdun is therefore the most powerful *point d'appui* for an attempt with a relatively small expenditure of effort, to make the whole German front in France and Belgium untenable. The removal of the danger, as a secondary aim, would be so valuable on military grounds that, compared with it, the so to speak "incidental" political victory of the "purification" of Alsace by an attack on Belfort is a small matter.'

The Crown Prince Wilhelm's Fifth Army, which had been opposite the Verdun sector for some months, was selected to carry out the attack. The Crown Prince had been considering the problem of Verdun for some time previously and with his Chief of Staff von Knobelsdorf felt that any operation against the fortress must be on a wide front and embrace both banks of the Meuse. As he later wrote 'we insisted that Verdun was the corner stone of the Western Front and therefore nothing less than an attack on a broad front could prevail against the forces that the enemy would certainly use

for its defence.' Falkenhayn was not interested in capturing Verdun, it would not fit in with his plans for a battle of attrition at all, and besides he felt that he did not have the divisions available to operate on a wide front. He insisted therefore that the Fifth Army must launch its attack from the west bank alone. Having ruled out the south and the west because of the unsuitability of the ground the Crown Prince decided on an attack from the north and northeast. To do this he had twelve divisions on an eight-mile front, a far greater density than the Allies had used in 1915, with a further three divisions in reserve. No less than 1,400 artillery pieces were to be employed from siege howitzers downwards. Wilhelm planned simply to punch a hole in the Verdun defences with his artillery and then push his infantry through the gap. This was to be done according to the principle of limited objectives, but at the same time his subordinate commanders were slightly confused by another order ordering them to maintain constant pressure on the defenders once the attack had started. This plan was given Falkenhayn's seal of approval on 6th January, although Wilhelm's concept did not quite fit in with his secret desire for a long-drawn-out battle. To this end he made sure that reserves, which Wilhelm was counting on being available on the first day of the battle, would be delayed in their arrival.

On the other side of the line the situation was not as happy as the Germans might have thought. In essence Verdun consisted of two lines of forts on a thirty mile circumference with the town of Verdun in the centre. Bombardments by German heavy siege artillery during 1915, unlike the effect on Liège at the start of the war, had caused little damage. Verdun could well be considered impenetrable. Unfortunately its 'teeth', in the shape of guns and men, had been stripped to the bone, to help Joffre's autumn 1915 offensive. The defence of Verdun had

been left in the hands of Chrétien's XXX Corps, consisting mainly of second line territorials. Pétain later described the situation thus: 'The forts rose silent and as if abandoned. Between the forts and beyond, there was only ruin: trenches largely caved in; barbed wire cut to pieces, its inextricable tangles covering the Côte de Meuse woods and the muddy Weovre plains; roads and tracks turned into quagmires; equipment scattered about, wood rotting and metal rusting in the rain.' One man, however, was perturbed about the situation. Emile Driant, an infantry lieutenant-colonel and a deputy, put out a warning to his fellow members of the Chamber of Deputies' Commission of the Army as early as 1st December and this reached the ears of Joffre who dismissed it as nonsense. Those actually present at Verdun began to notice the telltale signs of preparation for an attack in January, but little notice was taken by the French High Command apart from the sending of two further divisions to Verdun in February and mov-

Verdun, February 1916. A French stretcher party comes under shellfire trying to reach a fallen comrade

ing up of two corps to within supporting distance. They were misled by a series of German diversionary attacks along the whole French front between 9th January and 21st February and were thus showered with requests for reinforcements from everywhere.

The attack had originally been scheduled for 11th February, but bad weather forced the Crown Prince to postpone it and at dawn on the 21st the bombardment finally opened. Unlike the Allies the Germans went in for a fairly short bombardment. During the first five hours everything from the railway sidings in Verdun itself to the front line trenches was systematically shelled. A fair proportion of gas shells were used on French artillery positions in order to prevent counter-bombardment. The shelling then stopped and, as the defenders rose out of the ruins to prepare for the attack, the Germans, with their

71

German support troops move up to the front at Verdun. Note that compared to the standard British practice, their formation is open and irregular

highly comprehensive observation system, which included aircraft and balloons, were able to note which positions were still held. They then continued for another four hours, this time using their mortars against those parts of the line where the French had shown themselves. When the bombardment finally finished at 1600 hours, instead of putting in a mass attack, the Germans cautiously probed forward with fighting patrols and only on the right was any noticeable progress made.

For once the shoulder-to-shoulder principle would have worked. The bombardment had had the desired effect. The defenders were dazed, their artillery disorganised and their slender communications with the rear cut. The Germans would have had little difficulty in punching through

the defences and reaching Verdun itself. Surprised by the ease with which the probes had penetrated the French line Wilhelm ordered an all-out assault for the next day covered by a preparatory bombardment. The French, in spite of all, managed to put in local counter attacks before this attack went in, though without success because of their disorganisation as a result of the previous day. The Germans continued to move cautiously, still not quite believing that it could be so easy. They employed their flamethrowers (six companies worth had been allotted to Wilhelm) to good effect on strongpoints until the French saw how to get the measure of them by shooting down the pioneer who carried the bulky equipment before he could get within range.

25th February was perhaps the most serious day for the French. A small patrol of ten men of the 24th Brandenburg Regiment captured Fort Douaumont, the cornerstone of the French defences. On the same day Pétain was appointed to command the defence and he quickly brought order out of disorder. Forts were rearmed, sectors properly organised, new lines of trenches constructed and the supply system reorganised. On the first day of the battle the only railway into Verdun had been destroyed and the French were left with one narrow road as their communications with the rear. In contrast the Germans had no less than fourteen main lines to serve them, as well as a good road system, although the last twelve miles of the front were over very broken and arid country, which did present problems.

La Voie Sacrée (The Sacred Route) became the sole French lifeline. As Jacques Meyer, who fought in the battle, put it '. . . this "bucket conveyor" ran along the seventy-five miles of artery that brought to Verdun the generous blood of the reinforcements and carried back the exhausted troops and pitiable wounded.' The man who was responsible for running it, Major Doumenc, issued precise instructions that 'we will totally exclude horse or foot convoys, by shuttling them off onto parallel routes; finally, we will in no case interrupt traffic to make systematic repairs of the roadway . . . No motor convoys will cross it, but without being allowed to turn onto it . . . Any vehicle that cannot be towed off must be pushed into the ditch. No one has the right to stop, except for a serious breakdown; no truck may pass another.' Beginning on 29th February some 3,000 trucks carried 50,000 tons of munitions and 90,000 men towards the front each week. It was a masterpiece of administrative organisation and without it the French would un-

The remains of Fort Douaumont, the cornerstone of the French defences at Verdun, after the intense German bombardment

doubtedly have lost the battle.

As fresh divisions were fed into the mincing machine the fighting increased in fury. By the middle of March 'Verdun now meant hell. No fields. No woods. Just a lunar landscape. Roads cratered. Trenches staved in, filled up, remade, re-dug, filled in again. The snow has melted; the shellholes are full of water. The wounded drown in them. A man can no longer drag himself out of the mud.' Falkenhayn was beginning to realise exactly what he had committed his troops to, but there was no going back. On and on the fighting raged and by June even Pétain's nerve was beginning to crack and he suggested to Joffre that the French should pull back. Like Ypres for the British, Verdun had become a symbol to the French. The cries of 'on les aura' and 'ils ne passeront pas' had become watchwords, not merely for the defenders of Verdun, but for the whole French nation. In Joffre's mind withdrawal, however sensible it might appear strategically, was unthinkable and besides the Somme offensive was about to start. He was right in his decision for, on 11th July, in view of the pressure on the Somme, Falkehhayn called off the attacks. Pétain was now content to sit and recover, but not his subordinates, especially Nivelle and Mangin. From October onwards they conducted a series of fierce attacks aimed at regaining all the ground previously lost. Slowly they achieved this, with ever mounting casualties to both sides. Mangin, a tough soldier of the 'old school' who believed that the attack was everything, described his tactics as follows: 'I box in the first line with 75s; nothing can pass through the barrage; then we pound the trench with 155s and 58s (mortars) . . . When the trench is well turned over, off we go. Generally, they come out in groups and surrender. While this is going on, their reserve companies are pinned in their dugouts by a solid stopper of heavy shells. Our infantry waves are preceded by a barrage of 75s; the 155s help bang down the cork on the reserve companies; the tides of steel join up with the *poilus* [nickname for the infantry] seventy or eighty yards behind. The Boche gives up . . . You see, it is all very simple.' Simple it was; with no finesse the French were content to carry the theory of artillery power, as propogated by Foch at the end of 1915, to the ultimate.

The battle finally came to an end on 18th December, the French having regained almost all the ground captured by the Germans. The cost had been to the order of 350,000 casualties to each side. Falkenhayn had come close to utterly exhausting the French armies, as he had intended. He had not, however, in his original plan allowed for such casualties on his own side and this cost him his position. It

The Rimailho 155mm howitzer was the equivalent of the German 5.9-inch howitzer, and was the only really modern gun the French possessed among its heavy artillery at the outbreak of war. It had a particularly high angle of fire, and was thus very useful in trench warfare, where the more steep the fire of howitzers and trench mortars, the more valuable they were. This was even truer of heavy calibre weapons than of light calibre ones, as the former were effective against personnel and the entrenchments themselves, the latter against personnel, and only to a small extent against fortifications

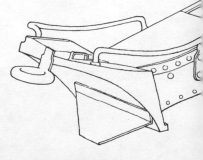

The French 58T trench mortar. *Weight of projectile:* 35lbs (with 13.2lbs of explosive). *Weight of whole apparatus:* 400lbs. *Elevation:* 45°-80°. *Range:* 500 yards. *Initial velocity:* 220 feet per second

Above: A French counterattack comes under heavy fire at Verdun. *Below:* Verdun: the legacy of the 'mincing machine'

is best left to Jacques Meyer to sum up the fighting: 'Verdun was most often a war of abandoned men, a few men around a chief, a junior officer, a noncom, even a simple soldier whom circumstances had shown capable of leadership. Sometimes it was a single man reduced to leading himself. Handfuls of men or individuals forced to act, to take the initiative of defence – or withdrawal. Failures of nerve – there were some – generally occurred in bigger units, which were not always the most hardened but were the most shocked by the unexpectedness of the disaster. Decisive and courageous acts were mainly individual, leaving most of them unknown.' Verdun, more than any other battle on the Western Front, was a soldiers' rather than a generals' battle.

Meanwhile on 4th March 1916 Haig had called a conference of his army commanders at St Omer, his headquarters. They were given their orders for the summer, and the task of attacking on the Somme was given to General Rawlinson and the newly created Fourth Army. Rawlinson had been given a warning order a fortnight before and had already done a reconnaissance of the ground. At the same time Plumer, commanding the Second Army in the Ypres Salient, was ordered to work out plans for an attack in Flanders. The news from Verdun was not good and it might well be that the British would be left to attack on their own. In which case Haig would attack in Flanders rather than the Somme, being still attracted by the idea of outflanking the Germans by capturing the Channel ports.

Back in his own headquarters Rawlinson viewed the problem with his corps commanders. The first task was administrative: the area behind the line must be adapted to cater for the wants of an army on the offensive. Everything from camps, light railways, store depots through to new roads and artillery positions had to be constructed. This gave the troops who were to take part their first inkling of what was in the wind. There is an entry in Jack's diary dated 29th April which says 'the Battalion finds large working parties under the Royal Engineers near the line nightly. Their tasks chiefly comprise the digging of communication and reserve trenches, constructing dug outs, carrying stores forward, bridging ditches for artillery, and repairing roads. Beside the Aveluy Road we see brand-new emplacements for heavy howitzers, dumps of shells and other stores, all carefully camouflaged beneath netting or roofs; while signallers are laying telephone cables on the ground everywhere. All this work, besides the receipt of voluminous instructions for training and organisation, points to a coming battle.' The mention of camouflage is interesting; the French were the first to take the art of disguise seriously and it was not until the Somme that the British began to concentrate on camouflaging positions with particular reference to the air. It was looked on as rather a joke to start with, as frequent cartoons of the time in the British magazine 'Punch' show. The noteworthy point about all these preparations, however, was that they were all completed in time for the assault.

Having got these administrative arrangements under way, Rawlinson then settled down to study his method of attack. By the end of March he knew that he would have seventeen divisions available and, looking at the ground, saw that the key lay in the Thiepval-Guillemont feature, which ran north-west to south-east, dominating the Ancre Valley. In order to secure this the flanks would have to be protected by subsidiary operations on the left around Gommecourt and the right in the Montauban area. With the divisions available this was just feasible, although the effort in the north would, to some extent, have to be handed over to the neighbouring army, Allenby's Third. To capture this position Rawlinson could either adopt the French doctrine of 'limited

**Overhead camouflage for a French
155mm gun on the Somme front**

objectives' or go for a bolder method.
The problem with the former was that,
by contrast with other parts of the
line, throughout a large part of the
sector the German second line was out
of range of the British field guns and
mortars. This meant that the guns
would have to be moved across trench-
ridden and shelltorn ground at a
critical juncture in the battle. Also
the enemy would have more time to
recover as Rawlinson was well aware
from a study of the French attempts
at this type of attack in 1915. The
bolder method reduced the attack to
two stages, first line and then second
line, by which time it was reckoned
that the breach would have been made
and the cavalry could be sent through
to exploit the situation. Rawlinson
was also convinced that a long 'softening up' bombardment was essential
for a variety of reasons. The German

wire was particularly thick in the
Somme sector, the Germans having
had plenty of time to prepare it in
what had previously been a 'quiet'
sector; it would therefore take time to
cut satisfactorily. The psychological
effect on the defenders would be
greater, especially if the long bombardment prevented rations from
coming up and wounded from being
evacuated. However he did not sacrifice surprise entirely for he planned
for the actual attack to go in at dawn.
  In spite of their ever mounting
casualties at Verdun the French were
still, as late as the beginning of May,
talking of providing at least twenty-
two divisions for the attack. Joffre
considered that his Sixth Army would
take the major role and that the
British task would be merely to '. . .
co-operate in the action of the French
forces, notably in facilitating their
passage of the river south of
Péronne . . .' He also wanted the
British to attack first in order to

draw off the German reserves, a proposition that Haig naturally shied at. Haig agreed that he would be ready by 1st June, but asked for four weeks warning of the date of the attack, which had now become somewhat flexible.

On 14th May the Austrians attacked in the Tyrol throwing the Italians back some eight miles. The Allied plan for simultaneous offensives on the three main European fronts was nullified. Joffre immediately told Haig that the attack must go forward on 1st July in order to take pressure off Verdun and the Italians. Haig, very unwillingly, in view of his worries over the training of the New Armies, agreed. At the same time he realised that the British would now have to bear the brunt and this was confirmed by Joffre at the beginning of June, when he admitted that Fayolle's Sixth Army would now consist of only twelve divisions. On 12th June Haig finally issued the operation order for the offensive. The object of the offensive, namely '. . . relieving the pressure on the French at Verdun and inflicting loss on the enemy', is important in that it explains why the battle was to take the form it did. There was no question of attacking in order to achieve a breakthrough; it might be considered as having purely negative aims. Admittedly the orders went on to lay down the method, which did talk about the action to be taken in the event of a breakthrough, but this was incidental. The offensive was to be nothing more than another 'wearing down' operation to force the Germans to release their grip on Verdun.

Haig's preparations for the battle included everything except preliminary attacks. Wirecutting, gas discharges, bombardment of communications and rest billets, smoke discharges and above all raids were employed to make life as difficult as possible for the Germans. These raids were not the impromptu affairs of 1915, but assaults in miniature using artillery and trench mortar supporting fire. During the period 19th December 1915 – 30th May 1916 the British had carried out sixty-three raids along their front. This was now stepped up and outside the battle area itself no less than thirty-eight took place in June. Whereas the main object previously had been to capture prisoners, these preparatory raids were meant to keep the enemy guessing as to where the attack was going to take place. In the actual battle area itself they were designed to check on the state of the German defences, and, towards the end of June, on the results of the preliminary bombardment. One important point which they failed to establish, however, was the depth of the German dugouts.

Falkenhayn had warned the German armies not engaged at Verdun that they could expect attacks and since he was unable to provide them with extra reserves they were advised to hold their front lines in the greatest possible strength and to defend each position to the last. There would be no question of adopting the normal technique of a more mobile defence since this relied on sufficient reserves being available to put in counterattacks. The Somme Sector was held by General von Below and his Sixth Army and in May he became convinced that he was going to be attacked. From his superior observation posts on the Serre knoll and below the Ancre the British preparations could be seen all too plainly. Consequently the Germans dug down and constructed a system of underground shelters complete with fresh air supplies. The chalklands of the Somme were ideal for this type of excavation. They also inserted machine-gun positions, many in concrete, to the rear of the front line trenches. Work also went ahead on a third line of defence some five miles to the rear. His Chief of Staff, Grunert, wanted to put in a preventive attack against the British, but the troops were just not available. German raids did much to help fill in the detail and a week before the attack the Germans were convinced that 1st July was the day.

On 24th June the bombardment started with a 15-inch howitzer sending a round chalked with a message 'A present for Von Stein's XIV Hun Corps' hurtling towards the German lines. For the next six days the Germans were subjected to a methodical bombardment from no less than 1,010 field guns, 427 heavies and 100 French guns – the munition crisis had finally been overcome. Yet the British did not have it all their own way. 'The German counter-bombardment is often heavy. We have suffered considerable casualties, and many parts of the trenches have been blown in; the field telephone lines also have been constantly cut.' The truth of the matter was that the artillery relied heavily on the Royal Flying Corps for correction of fire. Low clouds throughout much of the week hampered observation and it was the counter-battery work, which relied on accurate correction of fire, which suffered most. The constant raids reported the wire uncut in many places and this added to the concern of junior commanders in the trenches. Yet the morale of those about to take part remained high. For the volunteers of the New Armies this was what they had enlisted for and it made all those months of training under wet canvas in England worthwhile.

1st July dawned a fine day and as the gunfire on both sides rose to a final crescendo the assault troops prepared for the attack. At 0730 hours the guns lifted and all along the twenty-five mile front platoon commanders' whistles blew summoning all to brave the open wastes of No Man's Land. Once over the parapet, units shook themselves out into the laid down formation of extended lines, two to three paces between men and one hundred yards between ranks. Behind the assault waves came the supports and finally the reserves. On the German side: 'At 7.30 am the hurricane of shells ceased as suddenly as it had begun. Our men at once clambered up the steep shafts leading from the dugouts to daylight and ran singly or in groups to the nearest shell craters. The machine-guns were pulled out of the dugouts and hurriedly placed in position, their crews dragging the heavy ammunition boxes up the steps and out to the guns. A rough line was thus rapidly established. As soon as the men were in position, a series of extended lines of infantry were seen moving forward from the British trenches. The first line appeared to continue without end from right to left. It was quickly followed by a second line, then a third and fourth. They came on at a steady pace as if expecting to find nothing alive in our trenches.'

The day which had started with so much optimism turned out to be one of disaster. Along two-thirds of the front uncut wire and the German machine-guns held up and mowed down the advancing lines. From Gommecourt in the north down through Beaumont Hamel to Hamel itself, five divisions attacked on a five mile front and were back in their own trenches by the end of the day. Even the blowing of a huge mine in front of Beaumont Hamel did nothing to help success; the attacking infantry of 29th Division still followed orders to advance at the walk and hence were beaten to the resultant crater by the Germans. The three attacking divisions of VIII Corps, of which 29th division was one, suffered no less than 14,000 casualties. Small gains were made at Thiepval, where a brigade of the 36th Ulster Division actually reached the German second line but was forced to withdraw because the breakdown of communications precluded reserves being sent up to consolidate the position. Jack with the 8th Division south of Thiepval at the end of the day '. . . quitted the field on which such brilliant success had

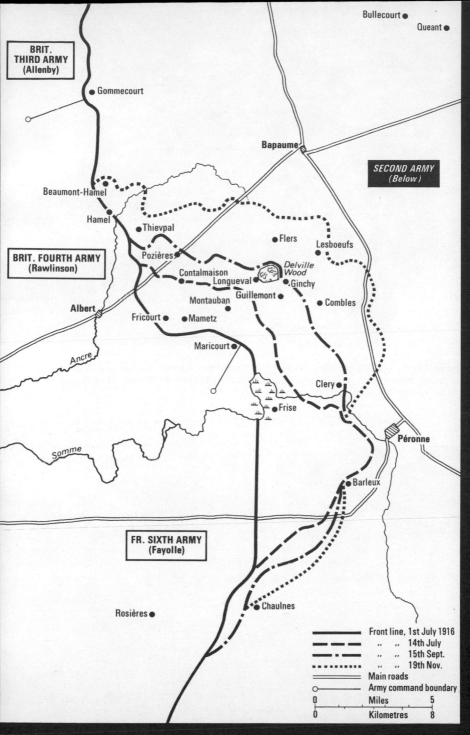

The Somme 1916

Above: 1st July 1916, the first day of the Somme. The 1st Lancashire Fusiliers fix bayonets prior to going over the top at Beaumont Hamel. *Below:* The Somme: a British Vickers machine gun crew in action

been expected that fine summer morning, leaving behind, dead or maimed, in that vast garden of scarlet wild poppies, some 90 per cent of the officers and about 60 per cent of the other ranks of the twelve infantry battalions of my division.' Their southern neighbours, 34th Division, suffered even worse losses with over 75 per cent casualties overall. Below them 21st Division and 7th Division attempted to take Fricourt by out-flanking the village from the north and south respectively and almost succeeded. It was just above the Somme however that the only reason-able successes were gained. Good ground observation of the enemy's defences and effective bombardments made for a straightforward task and the two right hand divisions of XIII Corps and the French XX Corps did achieve their first objectives. Below the Somme the five attacking divi-sions of Fayolle's Sixth Army also took virtually all their objectives. Again this was as a result of eight days' effective bombardment, but also because the French, with their greater experience of this type of attack, went for short rushes covered by fire as opposed to the parade ground method of the British.

The total British casualties on the first day of the Somme reached the staggering figure of no less than 57,470, of whom over twenty thousand had been killed outright. The British High Command took time to realise the nature of the disaster and one reputable war correspondent even went so far as to write: 'it is, on balance, a good day for England and France.' The fault lay partly in the lack of training and inexperience of the New Armies, but even more in the generals themselves, who had, with such little personal experience of the minor tactics of trench warfare, laid down the method of attack so rigidly. Only where units had taken the law into their own hands by advancing before zero hour and thus taking advantage of the cover that the bom-

bardment provided or had adopted the French idea of short rushes was there success.

Another mincing machine, like that of Verdun, had been set up and through the months ahead both sides were to adopt the same pattern of feeding fresh divisions in and then sending back the mangled remains to be fattened up for another attempt. Slowly the Allies pushed forward; Beaumont Hamel and Thiepval, which had been objectives for the first day, did not fall until November and September respectively. To the south of the Ancre progress was slightly better; Guillemont, Longueval, Del-ville Wood (which saw the decimation of the South African Brigade), Ginchy, and Lesboeufs were overrun, until by the 19th November when the battle finally ended the Allies had managed to reach the southern half of the Bapaume-Péronne road. The four and a half months fighting which it had taken to achieve this cost the Allies 630,000 casualties, the majority being British. The Germans lost about 660,000.

There were however important in-novations on the Somme. 14th July marked the first successful large scale night attack. (Festubert cannot be considered as one for the trenches captured were not held.) This was the attack put in on the German defences north of the Mametz-Montauban line. The plan was to deploy six brigades in No Man's Land during the hours of darkness in order to attack just be-fore dawn. Apart from normal har-rassing fire no special bombardment was laid on. This was Rawlinson's own brainchild, laughed at by the French, but it worked and showed that the principle of surprise had not been entirely forgotten. There was too, in August, the introduction of the creep-ing barrage. Instead of lifting to beyond the objective the moment that the infantry began their attack, the artillery fire moved forward in stages with the infantry moving up behind. This naturally took much careful and accurate planning, yet by the end of August this technique was successfully being used with the fire lifting fifty yards every minute.

The most striking innovation of all was the appearance of the tank on the battlefield for the first time. In February 1916, after Lloyd George, as Minister for Munitions, had given his blessing to the project, Swinton produced a memorandum which was to become the basis of tank tactical doctrine. He claimed that the tank would do away with the idea of limited objectives, saying that '. . . the Tanks will confer the power to force successive comparatively unbattered defensive lines, but, as has been explained, the more speedy and uninterrupted their advance the greater the chance of their surviving sufficiently long to do this. It is possible, therefore, that an effort to break through the enemy's defensive zone in one day may now be contemplated as a feasible proposition.' In order to allow the advance of the tanks to be unhindered the artillery should concentrate on counter-battery work since the enemy's guns would be the greatest threat to the tanks. Also the tanks were perfectly capable of tackling wire, machine-guns and earthworks on their own. He further suggested that aircraft could assist by dropping bombs on enemy gun detachments and concluded by saying that 'It seems that, as the tanks are an auxiliary to the infantry, they must be counted as infantry and in operation be under the same command.' Having shown it to the War Office and GHQ in France, Swinton then passed this paper to Hankey who, pessimistic at the idea of an Allied offensive in the west, felt that to have any chance it should be postponed until at least August so that there could be sufficient 'Caterpillars', as he called them, available. He also took up Swinton's idea of tank/air co-operation with General Henderson, the Director of Military Aeronautics, but it was not considered feasible. In fact ground attacks by aircraft were employed on the Somme, but it was not until later that 'grounding strafing', as it became called, was used to any extent.

Haig had been impressed by Swinton's paper and in April asked for some tanks to be available by 1st June for the start of his offensive. However, production on the Mark I had only just started and the crews had yet to be trained. He was all the same, rather optimistically, told by Swinton that seventy-five would be ready for him by August. In the event the first few tanks were not available for training until June and during August sixty were sent out. Unfortunately these had been sent out in such a hurry that the crews were only partially trained and the tanks themselves not mechanically proven. The British were about to fall into the same trap as the Germans with their use of gas. The temptation to try out a new weapon before it was available in sufficient quantities meant that any surprise gained would only have a limited effect, and would allow the enemy the chance to produce effective protective measures.

The British GHQ issued their first instruction on the employment of tanks in August. It laid down that they could be used in four ways: 1 the advance in line, which depended on large numbers; 2 the attack in groups or pairs against selected objectives; 3 for hauling guns and stores; 4 as mobile light artillery. Infantry were to co-operate closely with them and they should be preceded by an artillery barrage. Thus much of Swinton's doctrine had been understood, except for the employment of artillery with tanks. In the event because of the limited number available it was decided to adopt method 2.

In mid-August Haig had given Rawlinson orders to carry out a strong attack on a seven-mile frontage between Combles and Thiepval with a view to capturing the important communications centre of Bapaume and then rolling up the

Above: 'Duck yer nut' – graffiti on a gas alarm bell in the British trenches at Beaumont Hamel on the northern part of the Somme. *Below:* Canadian troops, so heavily-laden that they could scarcely run, go over the top during the Somme

**A British Mark I tank at Flers
September 1916**

German line northwards. Rawlinson's
first plan, which foresaw a three stage
attack on successive nights, was not
considered bold enough by Haig and so
his revised plan envisaged a total
breakthrough in the course of one
morning helped by the tanks. Forty-
nine of these were available and they
were allotted in roughly equal numbers to the three attacking corps with
a small reserve. On the night of
September 14/15th they moved forward to their starting points, but
mechanical failures accounted for
seventeen en route. The few that
actually came into action performed
well and one succeeded in capturing
the village of Flers (after which this

battle was called) together with 300
prisoners. The German reaction is
best summed up by the Chief of Staff
to Third Army Group, who on the
next day wrote 'The enemy . . . have
employed new engines of war, as cruel
as effective. No doubt they will adopt
on an excessive scale these monstrous
engines, and it is urgent to take
whatever measures are possible to
counteract them.' The German High
Command did not appreciate what
they were up against, and instead of
developing an anti-tank weapon, contented themselves with making suggestions of cutting wide trenches
across roads and digging tank traps.
The British Press had a field day and
allowed their imagination to run riot
as to the capabilities of the tank. They
were used again on 25th September,

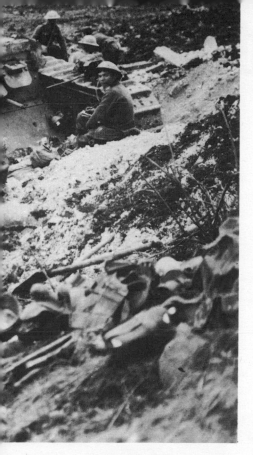

but by then few were still mechanically fit. Haig was convinced as to their potential and put in a demand for a thousand to be built.

The Somme battles had resulted once again in the most appalling casualties and the Germans, although they had been pushed back a few miles, had not had their line breached. Yet Haig's original aim had been achieved. The Germans had been forced early on to break off their attacks on Verdun and their army would never be the same again. As Prince Rupprecht of Bavaria put it: 'What still remained of the old first-class peace-trained German infantry had been expended on the battlefield.' With the weapons available at the time there was no way of breaking the deadlock and in view of the situa-tion on other fronts passive defence was unthinkable for both sides. If the German army had suffered, so had the British, and the loss of what has since been acknowledged as her 'finest generation', the volunteers who found their graves in Picardy, has been irreplacable. From now on they, like the other combatants, would have to rely on a conscripted army.

As to the survivors, it was to them the worst experience of the war on the Western Front. Those who are alive today would perhaps echo Gilbert Frankau, himself a gunner on the Somme, in this passage from his novel *Peter Jackson, Cigar Merchant*: 'The "Somme Offensive"! What remains of it today? Only memories, bitter memories that waken men o'nights; so that they see once more the golden Virgin of Albert, poised miraculously on her red and riven tower; Carnoy shattered in its hollow, a giant baby's toy-village, dropped from careless hand and smashed in the falling; the ruins that were Mametz and the ruins that were Contalmaison and the ruins that were Fricourt and the ruins that were Pozières; see once more the crowded horse-lines blackening Happy Valley, the balloons strung out like sausages across the sky, the thousand 'planes circling like hawks above them: so that they hear once more the staccato of machine-gun fire high in the air, the dull thump of the huge and hidden naval guns at Etinehem, the roar of squat nine-point-two's on their wheelless mountings, the roar of the railway-gun at Becordel, the thunder of eight-inch and six-inch howitzers in Caterpillar Valley, the ear-splitting crash of six-inch Mark VII's from the road by the Craters, the manifold clamour of the Archies (anti-aircraft guns) at Montauban, the constant bark of the field guns beyond: so that they walk once more, naked and alone, among the careless ghosts of men they knew, through that horror which was Trônes Wood . . .'

Backward steps

With the dying down of active operations in December 1916 the Allies could reflect that even if little progress had been made on the Western Front in terms of the recapture of ground, they had got on level terms with the Germans, who the year before had had much the better of the fighting. In view of this they were hopeful that 1917 would produce the total victory that was so badly needed. Meanwhile it was once again time for rest, recovery and planning.

The winter of 1916-17 on the Western Front was the coldest in living memory. The snow and frost lasted from October right through to the following April. Sickness in the trenches rose alarmingly and even a battalion like 2nd Royal Welsh Fusiliers, which prided itself on its low sickness rate, could report the staggering total of 134 men in hospital out of a trench strength of approximately 700 in February. In the British sector the tempo of raiding continued with a new novelty which had been developed during the Somme battles, the daylight raid. The frontline troops were beginning to dread this term. Captain Hitchcock of the 2nd Leinsters recorded that 'After a time these raids became unpopular with regimental officers and the rank and file, for there grew up a feeling that sometimes these expeditions to the enemy trenches owed their origin to rivalry between organisations higher than battalions ... Rivalry between formations is excellent, but when overdone can be most dangerous. The rivalry that existed in France in 1916 and 1917 over raiding operations, indeed had been carried to the extreme limit.' The Germans stepped up their efforts in this field and developed teams of professional raiders who operated up and down the lines like some travelling circus. These were to become the *sturmtruppen* of 1918. It was the Germans who can claim credit for the biggest raid of the war when, after a four hour trench mortar bombardment, they managed to inflict no less than 278 casualties on the British positions on Hill 60 on 9th April.

There was much greater emphasis on training than before. Schools of instruction in every conceivable aspect of trench warfare had sprouted up behind the lines and, if they did nothing else, at least gave the front line troops the chance to spend a few weeks in comparative comfort. Again, the French policy of using aged Territorials to garrison the front line during the quiet periods, had the advantage of allowing whole divisions to be withdrawn to rest and train for a particular operation, which they would then carry out before being withdrawn to their rest areas again. As Jack writes: 'Our infantry, on the other hand, are often given too few facilities for rehearsing their role in detail, and their energy is squandered on labouring tasks till shortly before attacking.' The British, who had up until now concentrated their training at company level, reduced this to platoon level. It had become apparent that in the narrow confines of the trenches the platoon of forty men was the maximum number which could be satisfactorily controlled. By now each platoon had its own Lewis Gun and much more emphasis was being placed on the principle of movement covered by fire – the French method of short rushes.

The Allied plan for 1917 had been originally worked out at the Chantilly Conference of November 1916 when Joffre had proposed that the offensive should be renewed as soon as possible. The French were to attack on a wide front between the Somme and the Oise, with a subsidiary operation around Reims, while the British made their effort between Bapaume and Vimy. These operations were scheduled to take place in February. Both the British and French Governments were unhappy at the lack of imagina-

A British outpost near Arras in the winter of 1916-1917, the coldest in living memory

Above: A British Lewis gun post. By 1917 each battalion had sixteen of these guns.
Below: A German attack with flame throwers, which form an effective smoke screen

tion shown in these proposals, especially in view of the heavy casualty figures from the Somme battles. The result was that Joffre was removed from command of the French armies and Lloyd George, who was by now the British Prime Minister, attempted, without success, to get rid of Haig.

Joffre's successor was General Robert Nivelle, who had come into prominence as a result of his successes in regaining ground at Verdun in the autumn of 1916. He was convinced that the techniques which he had employed in these limited attacks could be applied to a major offensive. There was, however, nothing radically new in them for they merely echoed the doctrine of maximum numbers of men and guns. They relied on the now dangerous assumption that a heavy and prolonged bombardment would destroy the German defences, thus allowing the infantry to walk across No Man's Land covered by a creeping barrage and break through with little or no opposition. He was convinced that, using this method, it would be possible to achieve a breakthrough within forty-eight hours and that there would be no question of a prolonged battle of attrition. This was what was attractive to both the French and British politicians, sickened as they were by the casualty figures for 1916, and by the beginning of January he had their backing to go ahead.

In essence his plan consisted of three stages. North of the Somme the British were to attack at Arras and Bapaume with Cambrai as their main objective and at the same time the French would attack at Roye, south of the Somme, with St Quentin as their goal. These attacks were to tie down the German reserves in preparation for the main French attack north of the Aisne, centred on Craonne, which would wrap up the German line northwards. The final phase was to be the exploitation of the British and French holding attacks, providing that the Aisne attack had been suc-

Nivelle, the 'born optimist' who succeeded Joffre as French C-in-C

cessful within forty-eight hours. His only other requirement was that the British should provide an extra six divisions in order to free French divisions south of the Somme for the attack. The operation was to be mounted as soon as possible after 15th February. Haig agreed to these plans on the understanding that a fourth phase should be added if the Aisne attack failed. He was still sold on the idea of an attack in Flanders, especially in view of the increased German submarine activity, which it was mistakenly believed was being directed from the Belgian ports. Hence Nivelle included a British attack in Flanders supported by the French, if the Aisne attack should fail. In the event it was not possible to start the battle on time because the railway system in the British sector was not working satisfactorily. Haig estimated that he required 200 trains a day to support his attacks and the Nord Railway Company were only providing him with 70. Nivelle therefore arranged that nothing should happen until this had been satisfactorily resolved.

By mid February, save for the railway problem, all seemed set for the plan to go into operation. However there now occurred something which was to set the plan off on the wrong foot. The continuous pressure on the German salient from Arras to the Aisne had, by September 1916, made the German High Command worried in the extreme. In Ludendorff's words they 'had to face the danger that "Somme fighting" would soon break out at various points on our fronts, and that even our troops would not be able to withstand such attacks indefinitely . . . Accordingly, the construction had been begun as early as September of powerful rear positions in the West . . .' By February these fortifications were approaching completion and consisted in the main part of a continuous line of defences running from near Lens in the north down to the Aisne, midway between Soissons and Craonne. This was called the Seigfried Line by the Germans and the Hindenberg Line by the Allies. A subsidiary line also ran from Drocourt down to Queant covering Artois and this was known as the Wotan Line. The characteristic of these lines was their depth and also their solid construction, mainly concrete. The Allies did not realise their extent because German air superiority in the winter of 1916-17 had prevented much reconnaissance behind the German front. Nivelle had been very open about his plan from the start and the Germans were expecting an early offensive. Consequently towards the end of February they began to pull back.

Since the defences were not complete the Germans withdrew slowly leaving strong rearguards to cover themselves on their way back. They also adopted a 'scorched earth' policy, leaving a trail of destroyed villages, cratered roads and innumerable booby traps and delayed action mines behind them, all of which slowed up the Allied advance. Besides this the appearance of open warfare after such a long spell of static fighting caught the Allies unprepared and the troops on the ground found it difficult to adapt themselves to the greater flexibility required. Thus the Germans were able to withdraw in their own time and it was not until the end of March that they were ensconced in the new line. They had now, although at the cost of surrendering a large area of ground, strengthened and shortened their line to such an extent that twelve less divisions were required to man it. Even more important they had thrown Nivelle's plan by nullifying both the Bapaume and Roye attacks, which left only the British effort at Arras in the first phase to contain the German reserves. At the start of the withdrawal the Allies naturally took this to be a sign that their efforts on the Somme the previous year had been worthwhile. But Haig later realised the effect that the withdrawal would have and concluded that 'the advisability of launching Nivelle's battle at all grows daily

less...' Not so Nivelle, who seemed to remain blind to this. More important to him was a French political crisis in March which brought down his two main supporters in the cabinet, Lyautey and Briand. Their successors, especially Painlevé, the new Minister of War, were against Nivelle, and his three army group commanders, Franchet d'Esperey, Pétain and Micheler were also losing confidence in the project. Success therefore became even more vital to Nivelle himself.

The German withdrawal had also delayed the start of the first phase and it was not until 9th April that the British were ready for their attack at Arras. The Canadian Corps was to assault Vimy Ridge, which had cost the French so many casualties in their 1915 attempts and Allenby's Third Army were to extend the attack southwards. Further south Gough's Fifth Army were to launch a diversion at Bullecourt. This time an even greater concentration of guns than at

Canadians dig in after their epic attack on Vimy Ridge in April 1917. The state of the ground shows the intensity of the preparatory bombardment

any time during the previous year was achieved. 1,106 were allotted to the Canadians, 1,773 to Allenby astride the River Scarpe and 519 to Gough for his diversion. The bombardment opened on the 4th, and in spite of the snowy weather and the continued German air superiority it was remarkably effective. The quality of the ammunition had improved and so had artillery fire planning. Besides this a new gas shell had been developed and this was used mainly against the German batteries, thereby considerably reducing their effectiveness. Particularly on the Canadian front, prior to the attack the front line was held with the minimum number of men in order to give the attacking troops as much rest as possible. The enemy was prevented from detecting this through frequent raiding. It had been hoped to have 240 tanks of an improved type, the Mark IV with thicker armour, available for this offensive, but in the event Haig had to make do with 60 Mark Is and IIs, none of which could keep out armour-piercing bullets, with which the Germans were now supplied. Once again Swinton's doctrine was ignored: the tanks were split amongst the attacking troops in penny packets. The Tank Corps Headquarters had also advocated that the preliminary bombardment should not be of more than forty-eight hours duration, but this was ignored along with other advice as to how the tanks should co-operate with the infantry.

The first day of the attack on the 9th brought some spectacular successes of which the taking of Vimy Ridge by the Canadians was the most prominent. Covered by a very precise creeping barrage, they carried all before them and by 1300 hours the ridge was in their hands. 'It was an extraordinary sight, a glimpse of another world. Behind them lay an expanse of churned-up mud and desolation completely commanded from where they stood . . . Below and beyond them on the German side lay a peaceful countryside with villages that appeared from a distance to be untouched by war.' More important, the reserves, who had been waiting in the tunnel and cave system below the ridge, were up in good time and the German attempts at counterattack failed. There was even an attempt to pass cavalry through them that afternoon to exploit the situation, but the torn up ground made it impossible for the horses to get forward. The eight tanks which had been allotted to them were all bogged because of the state of the ground, churned up by the continuous shelling, and hence the Tank Corps warning had been proved correct. The Third Army attacks reached the last line of defences before the Wotan Line and by the 11th were all set to penetrate this. Because of a communica-

tion failure the attacking infantry and the tanks with them found themselves advancing without a barrage, but succeeded in taking the village of Monchy-le-Preux some five miles short of the Wotan Line. Unfortunately two cavalry brigades sent up to pass through the gap were mown down by concentrated machine-gun fire. This was the first real chance that the horsed cavalry had had to operate as they wished and the lesson should have been clear that they were no match for well sited machine-guns, whereas the tanks had shown in the same action that they were capable of achieving success without the help of artillery.

By now the Germans had brought up their reserves and Monchy was the furthest point captured and held by the British. Gough's diversionary attack proved a failure. He had agreed to Tank Corps' pleas to mount an attack against Bullecourt without a preparatory barrage. Unfortunately he allowed too little time for the tanks to get to their jump-off positions and 'marry up' with the Australians and the first attempt on the 10th had to be cancelled at the last moment, but not before the Australians, who were the infantry concerned, had suffered casualties. A renewed attempt on the next day ended with disaster because the tanks were again late in arriving and the majority were knocked out before they reached the German first line by artillery fire and armour-piercing machine-gun ammunition. The Australians suffered heavy casualties and could not be persuaded to work with tanks again until the following year.

Nivelle's own attack in the south had been scheduled to go in on the day after the British, but he postponed it repeatedly by twenty-four hours at a time until the 16th, much to Haig's annoyance. The Germans had had every opportunity to prepare for this attack. He had issued details of it down to company level too far in advance and the Germans captured a copy of it on 6th April. They had plenty of time to organise their defences and, more important, their reserves, so that by the time the attack was launched no less than forty-two German divisions faced forty-eight French ones. Once again they kept their front line thinly held to avoid artillery casualties and relied on a mass of subtly sited machine-guns. The French artillery had fallen below that of the British in standard and there were too few howitzers, the only type of gun with the necessary elevation satisfactorily to destroy trench systems, for the forty miles of front on which Nivelle planned to attack. French staff work, as well, had not reached the British standard with regard to attention to detail and hence the fire plan and administrative arrangements suffered.

On 16th April the attack went in. Instead of the expected six-mile penetration nowhere along the front were gains of more than a mile recorded on the first day. The German machine-guns took their toll of the attacking waves, who found themselves held up by uncut wire and untouched defences. The French also had attempted for the first time to use tanks, but these arrived late and the infantry were too exhausted to go on with them. Besides they got bogged down and many became casualties to intense and accurate artillery fire. To the *poilus*, who had been told how easy it was all going to be, all this came as an awful shock and morale, which was not helped by constant flurries of snow, dropped sharply. In addition there was a complete breakdown of the medical services. In the wave of unreal optimism which dominated Nivelle's headquarters and caused slipshod staff work, the administrative plan had only catered for the very minimum of wounded and by the end of the first day the medical services could not cope, even though they had substantially raised the forecast figure on their own initiative. The following days were no more successful as the French struggled to get possession of the notorious Chemin des Dames Ridge, which dominated most of the sector. In order to help the French as much as possible Haig continued his operations around Arras, but it was of little avail.

The first signs of a crack appearing in the French army were on 3rd May when the 2nd Colonial Division refused to return to the line for yet another attack. As the month wore on and the attacks became more fruitless the mutinies increased. The feeling of the French units is well described by an NCO (Noncom) of the 128th Infantry Regiment. In spite of carrying out repeated attacks morale in the Regiment remained high until the middle of May, when an objective captured by them was lost by the relieving unit. They returned to rest billets and '. . . there, the men began to think about the insufficient support from our artillery . . . They realised that their sacrifices had been useless, perhaps even needless, and isolated, since the other arms had not properly supported them. There remained one hope, however; that of the much-needed and prolonged rest which the general had promised our regiment as a reward for its uninterrupted efforts in a fortnight's fighting. The men would also be able to resume going on furlough. But on 20th May the regiment was ordered back into the fireline. Gone was the hope of a good rest, gone the hope of leaves. The atmosphere became tense.' An exasperated regimental commander put it even more succinctly to Painlevé himself: 'This is a regression. We haven't learnt a thing. We are still sticking to the methods of 1915.' The French army had suffered such casualties in 1914, 1915 and 1916 that sooner or later they would reach their limit. That time had now come.

On 15th May Nivelle was sacked and replaced by Pétain, who brought the battle to an end on the 20th. By this time no less than sixteen army corps were infected with mutiny, their main cry being: 'We'll defend the trenches, but we won't attack.' Pétain acted immediately. On 19th May he issued his Directive No 1 to all his army group and army commanders. It was a secret document and stated that 'The balance of the opposing forces on the northern and north-eastern fronts does not for a moment permit of thinking of a breakthrough followed by strategic exploration. Therefore we must seek to wear out the enemy with the minimum losses to us.' In order to do this Pétain envisaged a series of limited attacks over a wide area using the maximum numbers of men and artillery available. No attack would be allowed to become too prolonged and this would thus prevent too great an indentation in the German line, which would lay itself wide open to counterattack. The object of this exercise was '. . . to grip the enemy and take away his freedom of action.' It was aggressive defence, in other words, that Pétain was aiming at. Besides the necessity to protect the battered French armies from any major undertaking another factor lay behind this policy.

The USA had finally entered the war on 6th April, exasperated by the start of the German policy of unrestricted submarine warfare. To Pétain therefore it was a question of holding on until the Americans could be brought across to Europe in sufficient numbers and as early as 17th April General Sir Henry Wilson, the Chief British Liaison Officer to the French headquarters, in a conversation with Foch understood that the French expected a year to pass before this could happen. Holding on could mean merely a passive defence, which the mutinous *poilus* were agitating for, but must be aggressive in order not to raise German suspicions that all was not well with the French. Haig was initially scathing about Pétain's concept, but this was at the end of April when he had only heard Pétain's ideas in outline and before the mutinies started to take place. In a letter dated

Pétain, French C-in-C after Nivelle was sacked in May 1917. Within a few months his firmness and humaneness had quelled the mutinies which were threatening to destroy the French army

29th April to the Chief of the Imperial General Staff, General Robertson, he sneeringly said that '. . . doubtless in his [Pétain's] mind he sees the British army doing the aggressive work, while the French army squats on the defensive.'

Thus the beginning of June found the Allies at a low ebb. The French army was on its last legs, German submarines were causing havoc amongst British shipping, the Austrians were counterattacking the Italians on the Trentino and the overthrow of the Tsar in March made the western leaders most pessimistic about any Russian contribution on the Eastern Front. There were only two encouraging factors, the first being America's entry into the war and the second, that the British army was still intact. The burden of operations on the Western Front now rested on Haig's shoulders.

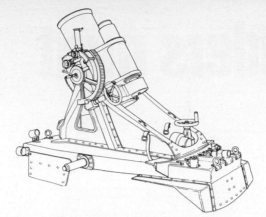

The German 25cm Minenwerfer Model 1912. *Calibre:* 25cm (9.84 inches). *Weight in firing position:* 11¼cwt. *Crew:* 21 (to carry the piece). *Rate of fire:* 20 rounds per hour. *Shell:* HE, 207.2lbs in weight. *Weight of charge:* 103.6lbs. *Range:* 219-601 yards

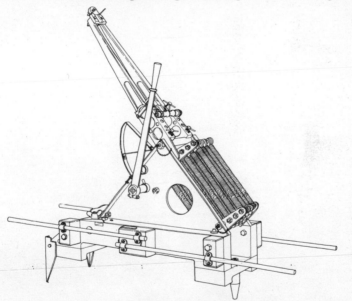

The West bomb thrower. Captain A West of the British army invented his bomb thrower in the early months of 1915, when the era of home-made trench weapons was in full swing, and officially commissioned designs had not yet reached production status. Although it was accurate and silent, it was heavy and expensive to make. The spherical bombs used were also expensive, and more important, difficult to produce, deliveries of the bombs thus being far behind requirements. The weapon was a catapult, the motive power being produced by twenty-four springs, and it was in this that the weapon had another major failing; the mechanism was much bulkier than that of the trench mortars by which it was succeeded, and the cocking lever protruded above the top of a standard trench, thereby betraying the position of the thrower. The manufacture of West bomb throwers was suspended in October 1915, and on 16th March 1917, GHQ in France ordered the destruction of all catapults in the British army

Flanders mud

Haig had been perturbed about the evident lack of success Nivelle's offensive had achieved practically from its inception. On 24th April he told Nivelle that its continuation had forced the British to continue their attacks at Arras to the detriment of the fourth phase of the original plan, namely the Flanders offensive. He argued that the Belgian ports could be captured indirectly if he continued his operations, but only indirectly, rather than by the direct approach through Flanders. It was therefore essential that the French should continue their attacks, not so much, one suspects to achieve a breakthrough on the Aisne, but to keep the Germans away from Arras. In other words it was time for the emphasis to be shifted from the French to the British attacks. What lay in his mind becomes clearer in an entry in his diary for 1st May: 'The enemy has already been weakened appreciably, but time is required to wear down his great numbers of troops. The situation is not yet ripe for the decisive blow. We must therefore continue to wear down the enemy until his power of resistance is further reduced.' He felt that Nivelle had gone wrong because he had tried to achieve a knock-out against an opponent whose guard was still strong. The wearing down attacks must continue throughout the early summer to make way for the decisive blow in Flanders before autumn. Haig therefore saw no alternative to the policy of attrition and Pétain's plan would assist greatly in this, provided that the French army was in a state to maintain an aggressive defence.

On 3rd May, Haig outlined his plan to Pétain. He explained that he intended to concentrate his troops opposite the Wotan Line (referred to as the Drocourt-Queant Switch Line by the

Allies) and the Hindenburg Line as far south as St Quentin, which anyway was the Franco-British boundary. While the French continued to carry on their operations on the Aisne he would then advance on this broad front. He explained his method as aimed at 'capturing and consolidating as much ground as can be prepared beforehand by our artillery. Then to push on advanced guards. At the same time we bring forward guns in preparation for another advance. The advancing troops will probably be held up but as the wearing out process of the enemy's forces continues, a moment will come when our advanced guards and Cavalry will be able to progress for much longer distances until a real decision is rushed [sic].' Thus it was a continuation of the 'Limited objective principle', although this term had now been more closely defined. Haig did not give any idea of the length of time he expected the Germans to hold on until the cracks started to appear. He asked Pétain to relieve six British divisions and to continue his attacks in order to contain the German reserves. The next day at a conference at the Quai d'Orsay both Prime Ministers agreed to the plan and it was accepted that from now on the British would bear the brunt. Pétain's only worry was over decreasing numbers of effective troops and he said that he would reply in writing to Haig as to the amount of support he could give. On 5th May, however, Haig changed his tune. In a letter to Pétain he introduced a new idea. The Arras-Vimy front would now become subsidiary to the main operation, which was to be the capture of the Messines-Wytschaete Ridge to the south of Ypres at the beginning of June. He would require sixteen divisions for this and its object would be '... securing the right flank and preparing the way for the undertaking of larger operations at a subsequent date directed towards the clearance of the Belgian coast.' Pétain was most un-

A German first aid post. The war which the planners expected would be over by Christmas 1914 enters its fourth year. The doctrine of attrition is destroying the flower of Europe's manhood

happy about this; as he said to Wilson, 'he did not believe in another Somme'. However on the 18th Haig met Pétain who, while unable to agree to the relief of the six British divisions, did offer a corps of four divisions to join the two French divisions already stationed on the coast. He also had four attacks in preparation which he would do his best to tie in with Haig's proposed dates of early June, July and August. Although Haig makes no mention of it in his diary, Charteris, his Intelligence chief, does note that Pétain said to Haig 'that the British as well as the French armies should confine their their fighting to small operations with limited objectives.'

In spite of Pétain's doubts, preparations went ahead for the Messines attack. Plumer, who had held the Ypres Salient with his Second Army for so long, had been given the task of capturing the ridge. Ever since January 1916 the British tunnellers had been hard at work driving six tunnels deep under the ridge and during the course of time some twenty miles had been prepared. It was a tense business and often the tunnellers could hear their opponents burrowing as well close to them. Once a German tunnel came as close as eighteen inches to a British one and then unaccountably veered away. The biggest problem was security and the Germans were naturally suspicious. They could see from the preparations that an attack was going to take place and stepped up the tempo of raiding to find out more details. They knew that mining was going on and mounted several raids for the express purpose of bringing back samples of earth thrown up by the diggings to determine the depth of tunnelling. On 9th April they did find some blue clay, which lay at a depth of between eighty and a hundred and twenty feet under the Ridge, the depth at which the

General Plumer, commander of the British Second Army, overtakes a French motor convoy

British were operating. They thought this was only an isolated example and disregarded it. One mine at Petit Douve near Messines was discovered and wrecked and at Spanbroekmolen it was calculated that a German tunnel would run into it on the morning of the attack.

A British prisoner captured in a raid on 29th May told the Germans that the attack would go in on 7th June after an eight day bombardment. This was correct. Plumer had left nothing to chance. Over 2,400 guns of all types were deployed to support the attack, roughly a gun to every seven yards of front. The bombardment started on the 30th and on the first few days concentrated on the German communication trenches, roads, camp areas and supply dumps. The air situation was dramatically different to that at Arras. Now the RFC dominated the battle area, enabling artillery spotting to carry on virtually unimpeded. As the 7th drew closer gas shells were introduced to force the defenders to

Germans suffer a gas shell bombardment

spend the maximum possible time uncomfortably in their gasmasks. Twice the bombardment rose sharply in intensity to make the Germans believe that the hour of attack had come. The German artillery was systematically engaged until by the time of the attack half of it was out of action.

The infantry who were to carry out the attack trained for it as never before. Twelve divisions had been allocated for the attack, nine for the initial assault and three in reserve. Each of the three corps taking part had constructed a training area behind the lines roughly similar to the ground over which they would be attacking. Plumer himself took a personal interest in the training and ordered a model of the whole battle area to be constructed. Seventy-two of the new Mark IV tanks had been brought up to assist, but their role was only a minor one, to assist in the cap-

101

ture of certain strongpoints. By 7th June it could be said that all involved down to the most junior rifleman knew exactly what his particular task was.

At 0310 hours on 7th June the mines were detonated. The sound of the explosions was heard in England. The attack then went in and within minutes the German first line had been captured. The mines had caused such shock and devastation among the defenders that they put up little resistance. The Germans attempted some half hearted counterattacks during the morning, but they were easily beaten off. In the mid afternoon the reserve divisions were passed through with their supporting tanks to take the German second line, which they did by dusk. Although the Germans attempted to regain their positions during the next seven days they were held and hence Haig had successfully completed the first stage of his plan.

Messines has been called by Liddell Hart '. . . almost the only true siege warfare attack made throughout a siege war.' It contained all the requirements for a successful attack: careful preparation, thorough training, surprise. Much abuse has been levelled at the British Staff in France during the First World War, but Messines coming on top of the success of Vimy Ridge illustrates what good work they could do. It must be remembered that the Staff of 1914 were relatively untrained and those of 1915 and 1916 had had no previous experience of handling the large numbers of troops and equipment that swelled the British Expeditionary Force from its original six divisions to sixty-two by May 1917. They had had to learn the hard way and Vimy Ridge and Messines showed how much they had learnt. The French Staff of the same time were not up to the same standard as has been seen at Chemin des Dames. Only the German Staff maintained a consistently high standard, but then they had been carefully nurtured in the years before the war.

There are only two aspects of the battle which detract from its success. Out of the seventy-two tanks which took part in the battle no less than forty-eight ditched. A report from the commander of the 2nd Tank Brigade stated 'The ground over which the tanks were operating has since been carefully examined, and there is no doubt that it was extremely difficult from a tank point of view. The chief obstacle was the marshy ground, and the fact that the bombardment had blocked many of the ditches, thus converting small ditches into a series of small ponds.' This was a dire warning of the problems that lay ahead for the second stage of Haig's plan. However one bright discovery was that the Mark IVs with their increased thickness of armour kept out the German 'K' armour-piercing bullets, which had been developed as a result of examining Mark Is captured at Bullecourt.

On the strategic level it has often been asked why Haig did not take advantage of this breakthrough and, using the principle of 'reinforce success', develop the battle further by making it his main offensive. Firstly, if we look back at his aim for Messines, it was only designed as a preparatory attack. However Haig had also considered the wider issue on the conduct of the war as a whole. In a letter to Robertson, Chief of the Imperial General Staff, dated 16th May he stated that he felt that the results of the intended Italian offensive against the Austrians were uncertain, as was the situation in Russia. This was what made him split his offensive into two isolated phases. He emphasised that the Messines phase was purely of a limited nature. As he wrote '. . . a decision will be obtained a few days after the commencement of the attack.' He went on to say that, in view of the Russian situation, if the Germans were able to transfer troops

An Australian trench on the Messines Ridge, June 1917. The soldier on the far left is wearing trench waders

from the East in time, which he thought unlikely, he would cancel the attack. He emphasised that the second phase would take place some weeks later and then only if '. . . the situation is sufficiently favourable when the time comes.' He concluded by saying that: 'It will be seen, therefore, that my arrangements commit me to no undue risks, and can be modified to meet any developments in the situation. Meanwhile they enable me to maintain an offensive proportionate to the forces at my disposal, which, in my opinion, is necessary in order to prevent the initiative passing to the enemy.' He was therefore 'feeling his way' and exercising caution instead of blindly committing his troops to the attack without regard to the consequences, a charge of which he has often been accused.

Flushed with the success of Messines Haig continued with his preparations for what was to be called the Third Battle of Ypres. An important part of his plan had been the assurance by Pétain that the French would carry out containing attacks over June, July and August. It was also this factor that had persuaded Lloyd George to give Haig a free hand. On 2nd June he was visited by General Debeney, the French Chief of the General Staff. What he had to say came as a shock to Haig, even though he was aware of the very low state of morale of the French army. Haig had expected the French to launch the first of their four promised attacks on 10th June, but Debeney explained that low morale had forced Pétain to send a large proportion of his forces on leave and hence this attack would not be able to be launched. However he did say that the next attack, scheduled for the middle of July, would take place. Haig was naturally upset but took solace in the fact that the Germans were counterattacking on the Aisne, which he hoped would swallow up their reserves.

A week later the British Government began to get 'cold feet' and a conference was called for 19th June at which Haig was asked to explain his plan for phase two and the reasons behind it. Lloyd George felt that the attack would not be worth the casualties likely to be incurred and felt that the only answer to the problem was maximum support of the Italians in order to knock Austria out of the war. Haig's answer to this is contained in an appreciation which he submitted on 12th June: '. . . To fail in concentrating our resources in the Western Theatre or to divert them from it would be most dangerous. It might lead to the collapse of France. It would certainly encourage Germany.' He added that it would discourage the British army and emphasised that results gained on the Western Front would be greater than elsewhere. It was the old argument of the Easterners versus the Westerners and there could still be no getting away from the fact that the bulk of the German armies lay in the West and Germany's strength lay in her army. However, Haig's greatest ally proved to be Admiral Jellicoe, the First Sea Lord, who at a session of the conference on 20th June, said that '. . . after this year we should not be able to continue the war for lack of shipping.' What he meant, of course was the German submarine campaign. Hankey, who was present, later thought that this statement was 'rigged', but it came as much as a surprise to Haig as to the others present. However it was the factor which caused Lloyd George reluctantly to agree to Haig's going ahead with the Ypres offensive.

Unfortunately, Haig, instead of attacking immediately after the successful action at Messines, now delayed. This was because he had decided to entrust the second and main phase to Gough and his Fifth Army staff. He felt that Plumer was too plodding and methodical, while Gough was by far the youngest of the five British army commanders and the most thrusting. It meant, though, that time had to be allowed for Gough's staff to become

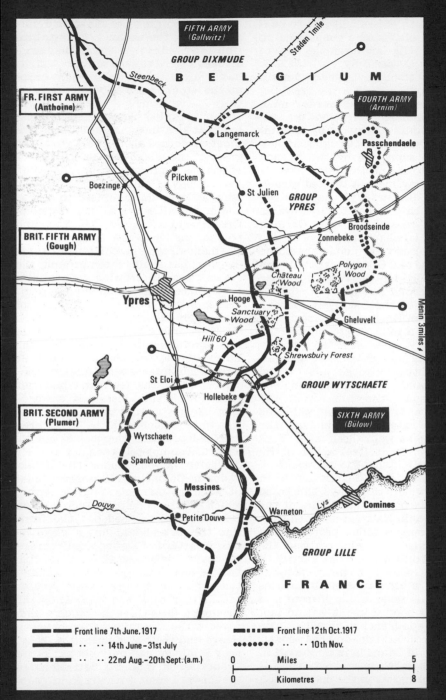

The Battles of Messines and Third Ypres (including Passchendaele)
June/November 1917

familiar with the salient and to concoct their plans. At a conference on 14th June Haig laid down the date of the attack as 25th July.

The plan itself envisaged two main attacks, by the Fifth Army breaking out of the salient eastwards and a semi-amphibious operation on the coast to capture Nieuport by Rawlinson's Fourth Army. Gough's attack was to be supported by two French divisions to the north while Plumer's Second Army made a limited attack from the Messines-Wytschaete Ridge in the south in order to tie down as much as possible of the German artillery. Haig had laid down that the limited objective principle should be maintained and Gough's original plan catered only for the capture of the German second line on the first day. This included the Gheluvelt Plateau and Pilckem Ridge, an advance of no more than a mile. There would then be a two day pause while the artillery was brought up and then the advance would continue. Gough got carried away and amended his plan to include the German third line, with the proviso that if things went well this would be extended to include the fourth line as well, three miles from the British front line trenches. He confidently felt that the key position, the Passchendaele Ridge would be in his hands within three days, this being five miles from the start line of the initial attack. Haig agreed with this, although not without protest from some of his staff, who realised the dangers of outstripping one's artillery support. Gough's artillery support consisted of 2,299 guns of all natures to cover his seven miles of front and the initial bombardment was to last ten days commencing on 16th July. Rawlinson's attack on the coast, which would be made in conjunction with the Royal Navy, was to be carried out '. . . as and when the main attack to the east of Ypres made progress.'

All the available tanks were mustered for the offensive and of the 216 produced a third were to be used for clearing strongpoints up to the second line, a third for the advance to the third line and a third in reserve. They were alloted a third to each of the two right hand corps, a sixth to the next corps on the left and a sixth to army reserve. Only the extreme left hand corps was without tanks. After their experiences at Messines the Tank Corps was most concerned about the state of the ground and once the bombardment opened they prepared a daily 'swamp' map, a copy of which was sent to GHQ, who, after a while, refused to accept them. As Fuller wrote: 'The fingers of the Steenbeck grew thicker and thicker, as the water dammed up in the main streams percolated outwards over the flat shell-beaten ground, the craters rapidly growing into miniature ponds, which in time melted together into a necklace-like string of diminutive lakes, until the Steenbeck itself became a long oozing moat of mud stretching from the north of the Polygonne de Zonnebeke, through St Julien, northwards past Langemarck.'

Meanwhile the Germans had not been idle. From Messines onwards they had known that a major offensive was to be launched in the Ypres area and had prepared themselves for it. They had completely remodelled their defensive lay-out under the supervision of Colonel von Lossberg, Chief of Staff to Arnim's Fourth Army, which held the Ypres sector. Von Lossberg had thinned out the front line troops and laid out a chequerboard pattern of strongpoints spread over a six defensive lines. Each line had its own counterattack force, and these became progressively greater the further back the line. Thus the Group Ypres of three divisions, which covered the five mile sector between Hooge and the Ypres-Staden railway, near Pilckem, had only six out of its twenty-seven infantry battalions in the forward zone, with six in the support line and the remainder behind the second and third lines available for counterattack. Behind the vital Passchendaele Ridge lay two specially

trained counterattack divisions. In all, to cover the sector, the Germans had nine front line divisions, backed up with six in immediate reserve, the two counterattack divisions and, to support these, a further three divisions. They had, in front of Gough's sector alone, 1,556 guns deployed and with the British artillery laid out with little cover on the exposed plain they were able to inflict maximum discomfort during the days immediately before the battle, in much the same way as they themselves had suffered before Messines.

On 7th July Gough had asked for an extension of five days for the bombardment to make more certain of success and Haig reluctantly allowed him three extra days. Then on the 21st Anthoine, commanding the French, asked for another three days and Haig thus set the date of the attack for the 31st. This extension was unfortunately to have the opposite result to that intended. Firstly the Tank Corps' 'Swamp maps' were giving a more and

Preparing for Third Ypres (often called Passchendaele): a British tankdrome, June 1917

more depressing picture of the state of the ground. Even more important, on the 29th and 30th, counter-battery work having started on the 28th, intermittent fog came down over the battlefield and hindered observation. On these final three days the assaulting infantry and tanks gradually moved forward and filed into the trenches. Behind them three divisions of cavalry moved up with the object, once again, of exploiting that elusive gap.

Dawn was breaking at 0350 hours on the 31st and General Jack, commanding a battalion of the West Yorkshire Regiment, saw '. . . the ground in front . . . lit up by bursting shells. To make sure, however, that they were ours, and not those of the enemy, I turned towards Ypres where I saw countless tiny gun flashes. Our barrage had opened; the inferno was deafening.' At that moment the assaulting waves were away following close behind the barrage. Because of the mist and low cloud the tanks had to be held back until daylight. The mist, however, helped the infantry, who were able to take the first line with ease. For the most part the tanks were able to catch up the infantry in time to tackle the second line.

Unfortunately it was in the attack on the second objective that things started to go wrong. The three divisions of Jacob's II Corps had been given the task of capturing the Gheluvelt Plateau, which was the dominant piece of ground in the battle area and hence the key to success. The line of attack was impeded by three woods, Château, Sanctuary and Shrewsbury Forest, and these contained narrow defiles between them. The going inside the woods was too bad for the tanks and they had to use these defiles, which were covered by the German positions. Of the first two echelons, comprising a total of forty tanks, twenty-two were knocked out and of the nineteen that eventually caught up the infantry all but one were destroyed by the German fire. This particular sector became known as 'the tank graveyard.' Elsewhere along the front better results were obtained and those tanks which remained unbogged provided great assistance in dealing with strongpoints. It was now, however, that von Lossberg's defensive system came into its own. By the time that the third line was being tackled the attackers had reached the extreme limit of their artillery cover and had only met a quarter of the German forces. In the afternoon the Germans counterattacked and the British were pushed back to the Steenbeck, the original assaulting divisions suffering heavy casualties.

Haig had wanted Gough to continue with his attacks, but not in the same thrusting way. '. . . I told Gough to continue to carry out the original plan; to consolidate ground gained, and to improve his position as he may deem necessary for facilitating the next advance; the next advance will be made as soon as possible, but only after adequate bombardment and after dominating the hostile artillery.' However the afternoon of the 31st had brought rain and this was to continue for the next four days making any idea of a resumption out of the question for the time being. Rain was to become the German ally and combined with artillery fire reduced mobility on the battlefield to a slow crawl.

Throughout August attempts were made to get forward, but always they became literally and figuratively bogged down. There were one or two bright spots in the general gloom, which showed that commanders were slowly learning. Before the war, Colonel Fuller had worked out a system by which infantry could advance in file as opposed to line. 48th Division calculated gloomily that to capture a few strongpoints around St Julien would cost them some 600 casualties, in spite of working with tanks. Fuller persuaded them to try his file system and the result was that the strongpoints were taken at a cost of only fifteen killed and wounded. This was a timely experiment for on 14th August, Fifth Army had issued a report in which it was stated that tanks '. . . are slow, vulnerable and very susceptible to bad "going". The "going" on a battlefield will always be bad . . . it would appear that the moral effect of their appearance is diminishing rapidly.' Fuller then went on to write a memorandum on 'Minor Tank and Infantry operations against Strong Points' in which he laid down: '. . . The object of the tank is 1 To force the enemy to seek shelter from its fire and so deny him the use of his weapons; 2 to distract the enemy's attention from the infantry attack; and 3 to hold the enemy in his shelters until the infantry come up and capture him. And [that] the object of the infantry is; 1 To kill and capture the enemy; and 2 to hold the position once it has

Above: Tank versus flame thrower. The crew of this British tank were burned to death when their fuel tank was ignited by the flame thrower. *Below:* Manhandling a British 9.2-inch howitzer through the mud of Third Ypres

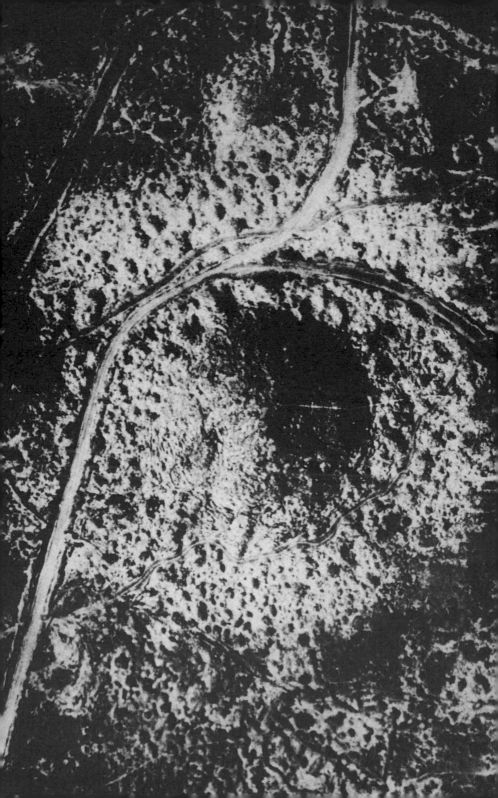

been captured.' His idea was for the tanks to advance in the company of infantry scouts, who would form the link between both. The main body of infantry would advance in file behind the tanks with light machine-gun teams placed between the files. The whole would be supported by a medium machine-gun barrage. These tactics were accepted by the Fifth Army. The other point was that it at last dawned on commanders that heavy bombardments were assisting the Germans more than the British by cutting up the ground so badly. This is well illustrated in an extract from a XIX Corps Artillery Operation Order for an attack in September. 'The intensity of the preliminary trench bombardment will for the future be materially reduced. To cover the whole country with a mass of shell-holes seems to be playing the enemy's game and merely tends to help him in his present tactics.'

With the disappointments of the initial attacks Rawlinson's amphibious operation was shelved, which pleased Rawlinson himself, being a believer in the theory of the limited objective. Gough became very depressed at the failure of his plans and even suggested closing down the offensive altogether. Plumer advocated the maintenance of pressure on the Germans and gradually the emphasis shifted from Gough back to Plumer who, after all, was the expert on the salient. At home Lloyd George and the Cabinet still hankered after switching the emphasis to the Italian Front and Haig was persuaded to give up some heavy artillery for this purpose. The French, meanwhile, were doing their best to support Haig's efforts with diversionary attacks elsewhere.

The Third Battle of Ypres consisted of three distinct stages, of which Gough's opening attempts at an immediate breakthrough constituted

The area around the Ypres-Comines Canal, pock-marked with innumerable shell holes

the first. The second phase was the pursuit of the limited objective doctrine and consisted of Plumer's attacks on the Menin Road Ridge (20th September), Polygon Wood (26th September) and Broodseinde (4th October). They carried the stamp of Plumer's particular brand of careful preparation and planning which had made Messines such a success. Having captured an objective the infantry immediately consolidated, however tempting it was to push on immediately. The artillery were moved forward and in this way the German counterattacks made no headway. There is no doubt that the Germans soon lost the complacency they had shown in August. The weather had dried out and nothing they did seemed to produce an effective counter. They realised that their blockhouses were too tempting as artillery targets and now conducted their defence from shell-holes. Their artillery economised by concentrating at the decisive point and at Broodseinde they tried to forestall the British attack by attacking themselves, only to be caught in No Man's Land by the British barrage. The German accounts of these actions portray not so much concern at losing ground but rather at the heavy loss of men. The German official monograph called Broodseinde 'the black day' and Ludendorff said of it 'we came through it only with enormous casualties.'

Much of the brunt of this second phase fell on the Dominion troops, in particular the Australians, who brought their own brand of dash to the battlefield. There is no doubt that there had been a sharp deterioration in the British divisions during 1917. The coming of conscription had produced a lowering in spirit, as compared with the Kitchener formations of the year before. Sir Phillip Gibbs, whose despatches from the front were famous, wrote that 'for the first time the British army lost its spirit of optimism.' In September this showed itself all too plainly when at the Infantry Base Depot at Etaples such serious rioting took place that two battalions, 1st Battalion Manchester Regiment and 1st Battalion Honourable Artillery Company, had to be withdrawn from the battle to deal with it. Undoubtedly much of this had to do with unsympathetic handling by those in charge of the depot. All drafts from England were sent to these depots before being sent up to units in the line. They were put through a rigorous programme of training, which was resented by many of the veterans. What galled most however was that they were not allowed to leave their camps and this resentment, combined with a low opinion of their instructors, many of whom had had no front line experience, eventually broke out into what seemed to be likely to become another French mutiny. The Dominion troops, with their different and more relaxed ideas on discipline and, more importantly, the fact that they were all still volunteers, produced better results in action and began to be relied on more and more to bear the main burden. This is not to say that all British divisions were tarred with the same brush; many maintained a high-reputation throughout.

The final stage of the battle is the one that has been most criticised by historians. This involved the battles of October and the beginning of November to capture the Passchendaele Ridge, the original aim of the first phase. In fact the general public wrongly calls the whole offensive by this name. After the successes of the second phase the weather suddenly deteriorated again. Haig has been much slated for even contemplating attempting this third stage in the almost impossible ground conditions which the heavy rains had brought about. Even some of Haig's subordinates advised against the idea. There was one major reason why he did carry out these attacks and that was the nature of the Passchendaele Ridge itself. If Haig was to stay where he was below the ridge for the winter he would be condemning his troops to a

most uncomfortable time in what would be a most vulnerable position. Thus attacks were continued in worsening conditions, until by mid-November the village of Passchendaele, along with part of the ridge, were in British hands. This was not wholly satisfactory, for the Canadians, who had taken the major role in these last few attacks, were left in a very dangerous salient. The sheer physical impossibility of moving further forward, because of the mud, together with an urgent request to ship troops to the Italian Front after the catastrophe of Caporetto forced Haig to bring operations to an abrupt halt.

On the surface, Third Ypres produced little better return than any of the previous offensives. In three and a half months a maximum penetration of five miles had been made in the German line. The Official British History puts British casualties at 244,897 and the Germans' at approximately 300,000. Yet in wider terms it was important. Firstly the pressure was taken off the French, giving Pétain time to implement his reforms, until by the autumn, as we shall see, the French army was able to regain its self-respect and take its place again as a viable fighting force. Equally important was its effect on the Germans. The German Official History says: 'Divisions disappeared by dozens into the turmoil of the battle, only to emerge from the witches' cauldron after a short period, thinned and exhausted, often reduced to a miserable remnant.' The History goes on to accept that the British offensive succeeded in protecting the French, but states: 'Above all, the battle led to an excessive expenditure of German forces. The casualties were so great that they could no longer be covered, and the already reduced battle strength of the battalions sank significantly lower.' If, therefore, Third Ypres is regarded as a battle of attrition, the British had come off significantly better from it, but then,

with the Americans starting to arrive in France, they were about to have greater resources to draw on than the Germans. In the long run it did considerably help to finish the war in 1918, whereas if Pétain's idea of waiting for the Americans had been followed the war would have certainly lasted well into 1919. Unfortunately it exhausted the British army to such an extent that it was to be given a considerable fright in the spring of 1918. Also the mistrust between generals and politicians which grew up as a result of the battle was also to create problems

German dead in a captured trench

during the next year.

On the tactical side it had shown that the limited attack could eventually bring about victory, provided that there was sufficient artillery, careful planning, good weather and firm going. Equally it showed that this method would never produce a quick decision. Yet before the year was out some dramatic experiments were to take place which would pave the way for quicker methods.

Blueprints for Victory

While the British were locked in battle in Flanders Pétain had been busy carrying out a radical reorganisation of French methods. In his Directive No 1 of May 1917 he had laid down his overall methods, together with directions on how to stop the rot in the French Army. Using, like Haig, the doctrine of the limited attack as the basis of his tactics, he went on to develop his ideas in his Directive No 2, dated 20th June.

No longer would the French expose their infantry to an attack en masse. In future the theme would be maximum artillery and minimum infantry. At the same time training would be stepped up and whole formations would be taken out of the line to spend time in training camps to the rear. In particular Pétain emphasised the value of co-operation between the various arms, infantry, artillery, aircraft and new weapons like tanks. This he hoped would produce new methods for attack and defence.

He followed this up a fortnight later with Directive No 3 which concentrated on reorganisation. For a start the French defences were going to be manned in greater depth, but with greater rotation of units between the front line and reserve. He also set about building up a central reserve and set its staff at working out elaborate movement tables so that it could be sent to any part of the front in the minimum possible time. The staff was reorganised so that the *Deuxième Bureau* (Intelligence) and the *Troisième Bureau* (Operations), who up until then had regarded one another with jealousy and loathing, would work more closely together. Experts in air and tank matters were appointed to the Staff and the rigidity and careless thinking of the past was transformed.

Above all Pétain reorganised the Artillery. Each Corps received a much greater allocation of guns, with special emphasis on heavy natures. This showed what a deep impression the German artillery strength at Verdun had made. Aircraft, balloons and tanks were also allocated in increased amounts. Pétain had become a great believer in air power, more so than the British. Whereas artillery spotting remained an important part of air co-operation, 1917 showed a gradual transition from straightforward reconnaissance to a new role of ground attack by aircraft, which had been first mooted by Colonel Swinton for use with tanks.

Pétain carried out three experimental attacks using his new methods. Firstly he increased the support for the six divisions of Anthoine's First

General Guillaumat, commander of French Second Army in an artillery dominated attack in August 1917

114

Army, which was fighting alongside the British in Flanders, to 300 heavy and medium guns, 240 field guns and 200 aircraft. During the first phase Anthoine did all that was asked of him, although he wanted a longer bombardment than Haig had originally planned for. His later results were not so successful, but at least it had proved that French troops had regained their offensive spirit. Then, on 26th August Guillaumat's Second Army launched an attack in the Verdun sector to capture the commanding ground to the north of the town. The new doctrine was perfectly illustrated, the gunners outnumbering the infantry by six to four. An advance of 4,000 yards on an eleven mile front was envisaged. Preceded by an eight day bombardment the attack was a copybook success. Finally, at Malmaison, west of the Chemin des Dames Ridge, Maistre's Sixth Army put in the same type of attack on a seven mile front on 23rd October, preceded by a six day bombardment. Again complete success resulted and the German position on the Chemin des Dames Ridge was turned, causing the Germans to evacuate it. Yet it must be emphasised that Pétain was not concentrating on a new method for a major offensive. Unlike the second phase of Third Ypres, these two attacks consisted of one limited stage only and were very much in accord with his overall doctrine of merely keeping the Germans occupied until the Americans could mass sufficient strength in France.

Pétain's doctrine was almost wholly defensive and much of it was formulated as a result of a study of German defensive methods. He noted particularly the ever increasing emphasis that the Germans placed on immediate counterattack and in particular the von Lossberg defence doctrine. The importance of defence in depth and, especially, the need to keep one's counterattack troops well back at the expense of surrendering ground, stuck in his mind. The idea of voluntarily

116

giving up ground would have been sacrilege in 1916 and would have negated the whole spirit in which the Verdun battle was fought. Small wonder then that it took Pétain some time to get his ideas accepted by his subordinates. As regards the attack the French also noticed, as a result of German operations in the Chemin des Dames sector in July, that the Germans were beginning to do away with the long preparatory bombardment in favour of a short five minute affair immediately before the attack went in, which gave the defenders too little time to climb out of their dugouts and man the fire-step. This all came from a German pamphlet produced in August entitled 'Instructions on the counterattack in depth', which Pétain had translated and circulated throughout the French Armies. In particular it showed that the German stormtroops were not a permanent formation, but were merely selected from amongst normal units in accordance with the situation at the time. Pétain's deductions were collected together in his Directive No 4, which was not issued until towards the end of December when it was known that the Germans were planning to go on to the offensive early in the new year.

The Germans themselves had been working on a new method of attack. They had developed a new form of gas, which had first been employed on 11th July in front of Ypres. They called this Yperite. The first gas used had been chlorine and then bromine or 'K' gas had been introduced on the Somme. (This was a choking gas which affected the lungs. However it would only affect those in the immediate vicinity of the exploding shell and even then only if they were not wearing masks.) Yperite was phosgene and soon came to be known as Mustard Gas, after the smell. It was mainly a blistering agent and caused severe vomiting as well. Its advantages were that one part in 4,000,000 of air was sufficient to cause blistering and hence it was eminently suitable for artillery shells. By put-

Russian gas casualties in a German field dressing station

ting a small container inside an HE shell a dual effect of gas and high explosive would result and the explosion would disguise the gas thereby taking its victims unawares.

The Germans tried this out as an offensive weapon against the Russians at Riga on 1st September. This was one of the German operations aimed at forcing the Russians, after the disasters of their June 1917 offensive, to sue for an armistice. General von Hutier's Eighth Army attacked on a narrow front of only 4,600 yards after a combined HE and gas bombardment of only five hours. Infiltration tactics were used and the whole battle was over within a few hours, leaving the Russian defenders streaming back eastwards in panic. Admittedly Russian morale was very low, but it showed that there was something in trying to incapacitate the defenders rather than the defences.

Flushed with the success of this experiment the Germans determined to use it on a larger more decisive

scale. The Austrian General Conrad von Hötzendorff, sometime Austrian Chief of Staff until his dismissal in February 1916 and now commanding an army group on the Italian Front, had suggested to Ludendorff that the time was ripe for a joint Austro-German offensive aimed at knocking Italy out of the war. Ludendorff responded to this by transferring von Below's army of seven divisions from the Russian Front. On 27th October at 0200 hours a six hour bombardment opened using the same mixture of gas and HE as at Riga. The attacking troops then went in and at the end of the first day the Italians had been driven back ten miles in complete disorder. Again the tactics of infiltration were employed in locating the gaps in the defences, enabling these to be exploited in the minimum of time. The headlong flight of the Italian army did not stop until the River

General Conrad von Hötzendorf, Austrian *Gruppe* commander on the Italian front

Piave had been reached, eighty miles to the rear. The disaster of Caporetto cost Italy 800,000 casualties and forced five British and six French divisions to be transferred at very short notice from the Western Front. Ludendorff was now sure that he had a blueprint for victory.

The British too were about to experiment with a new form of attack. As early as 2nd August Colonel Fuller had thought that the Flanders offensive, at least as far as tanks were concerned, was still-born. He produced a paper the next day suggesting that a joint force of two British and two French divisions should capture St Quentin with a view to restoring 'British prestige' and striking '. . . a theatrical blow against Germany before the winter'. General Elles, commanding the Tank Corps, felt that this would not be accepted by GHQ and the plan was watered down to a large wholly British raid in the area of Cambrai. Fuller then produced a paper on 'Tank Raids' and he saw their object as being 'to destroy the enemy's personnel and guns, to demoralise and disorganise him and not

118

to capture ground or to hold trenches'. they were, in effect, to be a large-scale version of the ordinary trench raid. Instead of merely a company of infantry being employed he saw each raid consisting of six battalions of tanks, two infantry or cavalry divisions with supporting artillery along with two squadrons of aircraft, medium machine-guns, extra field artillery, engineers and tracked gun carriers mounting medium artillery pieces. The tanks were to attack in three waves, the first to take on the enemy artillery, the second to deal with wire and trench systems and the third to make for 'special tactical points'. The infantry or dismounted cavalry were to work with the second line of tanks and the aircraft were to attack the enemy infantry and artillery and disrupt his lines of communications. Much of the artillery would be employed in laying smoke barrages to the flanks, whilst the medium and heavy artillery would concentrate on counter-battery work and shelling the enemy approaches. 'The essence of the entire operation is surprise and rapidity of movement. Three hours after zero the retirement might well begin, the tanks and aeroplanes acting as a rearguard to the dismounted cavalry retiring with their prisoners . . . The spirit of such an enterprise is audacity, which should take the place of undisguised preparation . . . We must abandon the obvious and rely on surprise and the unexpected.' He made the point that there was no reason why five or six of these raids should not be carried out before the following spring with a view to so demoralising and bewildering the enemy that eventually one of them might be replaced by a decisive battle.

General Byng, commanding the Third Army, in whose sector Cambrai was, was much taken with the idea, but it was not until 13th October that Haig himself sanctioned it. The reason for the delay can be seen in a letter that Haig wrote to Sir Eustace Ten-

nyson D'Eyncourt, who had been connected with tank design from the beginning, on 27th August. He pointed out that the tank alone could not dictate where a battle was to be fought, since it was still in its infancy and mechanically unreliable, which meant that troops would not be prepared to sacrifice artillery support in lieu. 'In its present state of development the tank is an adjunct to infantry and guns, although undoubtedly a valuable one under conditions favourable to its use.' The tank was, in his eyes, a useful supporting weapon but could never be considered a decisive weapon in its own right.

Regrettably, the plan, when it was finally evolved, proved very different from Fuller's original idea. Instead of being a mere raid it had now turned into a full-scale offensive with distant objectives. Having broken through the Hindenburg Line between the Canal de L'Escaut and the Canal du Nord, the cavalry were to sieze Cambrai and the

British tanks (still considered by Haig to be useful weapons but not decisive in their own right) wait to advance in the Battle of Cambrai, November 1917

crossings over the River Sensée beyond, while the infantry and tanks secured the Bourlon Ridge. Exploitation would then take place north-east to Valenciennes, thereby rolling up the German front. To do this there were allotted six infantry divisions, nine tank battalions, five cavalry divisions and a thousand guns. When Fuller saw this he was aghast '. . . because on August 4th, I had selected this area of attack on account of it being advantageous to a raiding operation and disadvantageous to one of decisive intention'. The only reserves appeared to be mounted cavalry and Arras had shown how ineffective the mounted horseman was against machine guns and barbed wire. On the credit side the country was ideal for tanks, being gently rolling chalk downlands, which would drain easily. Also Byng had laid down that there would be no preliminary bombardment. Guns were to be laid using new survey methods and registering of targets would hence not take place. Fuller devised special tactics for penetrating the Hindenburg Line, making use of smoke barrages to the front and flanks, getting the infantry to adopt his single file method of advance and constructing fascines of wood to enable the tanks to cross the extra wide trenches. The only major snag to the initial phase was that Byng insisted on using almost all his tanks at the start, leaving only a company in reserve. Secrecy was of prime importance and all movement of tanks took place by night. The security was so good that the Germans only became suspicious in the last twenty-four hours before the attack, having captured two prisoners in a raid near Havrincourt who admitted to having seen tanks in the area and, also, having tapped a telephone conversation between two artillery signallers (an embargo had been placed on all infantry telephone lines).

20th November, the day of the attack, dawned misty, much as it had for the Germans at Riga and Caporetto, and at 0620 hours the artillery opened fire and at the same time six divisions of infantry preceded by 378 tanks, led by General Elles himself, moved out into No Man's Land. Overhead no less than 289 aircraft set about a systematic ground strafing of the German positions, as well as making sure that there was no interference from the German air force. Almost everywhere the plan worked like clockwork and by nightfall an advance of up to five miles had been made on a seven mile front with 8,000 prisoners and 100 guns captured. Unfortunately two conditions had failed to materialise. The Flesquières Ridge, which lay directly in the path to Cambrai, remained in German hands, causing a sharp indentation to the new British line. More than anything

else this had been caused by German artillery batteries which had accounted for no less than sixteen tanks as they topped the ridge. This produced an important lesson in infantry tank cooperation, which still holds good today. Haig quite rightly deduced in his diary that: 'This incident shows the importance of Infantry operating with Tanks and at times acting as skirmishers to clear away hostile guns and reconnoitre.' Yet on examination of the battlefield afterwards it was noted that the infantry, who were of 51st Highland Division, were unable to get forward as they were pinned down by the fire of a mere three machine-guns. If cooperation had been working correctly the tanks would have dealt with the machine-gun nests first and then the infantry in turn would have taken on the artillery. This was acknowledged by Fuller in his report of lessons learnt from the battle. The other aspect, which was more serious, was the inability of the cavalry to move forward to exploit. Instead of being

placed under command of the two infantry corps involved they remained under command of the Cavalry Corps. The hold-up at Flesquières led them to believe that their moment had not arrived and apart from an isolated action by a squadron of the Fort Garry Horse in capturing a battery of guns the whole five divisions remained inactive. By the time the attack was resumed the next day the majority of the tanks were disabled and only some forty could be got into action. The folly of leaving such a small reserve was now proved. Flesquières Ridge had been abandoned by the Germans, but from now on the advance became a more traditional slog as the Germans, with their usual quick reactions, brought up more and more reserves.

By 30th November the advance had progressed another two miles. Bourlon Wood was inside British lines but Cambrai still lay three miles away. If there had been further reserves the results might have been different, but Haig, as he admitted in his diary entry of 27th November, had none to give.

Cambrai, the first day: British infantry with a stretcher and a Lewis gun follow up the breakthrough made by the tanks

Unfortunately his complacency had got the better of him in his belief that the Flanders campaign had swallowed up all the German reserves. He believed that, except about Bourlon Wood, the enemy was thin on the ground. This could not have been further from the truth as was shown on 30th November when the Germans launched one of their new-style attacks, catching the majority of British troops unawares and pushing them back a distance of up to five miles.

The Battle of Cambrai is noteworthy, not so much for showing what could be done with the tank, but more because it produced the tactics that the Germans were to use in their 1918 offensives and those that the Allies were to use in the late summer of that year. C S Forester has likened the generalship on the Western Front to a '. . . debate of a group of savages as to

The German counterattack at Cambrai. Their use of infiltration tactics was a harbinger of their resounding successes in early 1918

how to extract a screw from a piece of wood'. Having tried to pull it out in various ways that enabled more force to be applied 'they could hardly be blamed for not guessing that by rotating the screw it would come out after far less effort'. The Germans and the British had come up with two methods of 'rotation' which had certain similarities. Both relied on new weapons of war, gas and the tank. They had both got away from the idea that artillery was the major weapon on the battlefield, yet at the same time appreciated the need for the attacking troops to tackle the enemy artillery as the first priority. Yet they differed in the fact that the Germans reinforced success while the British reinforced failure. It had been amply proved at Caporetto that there was no need to capture all of one's objectives so long as one did find gaps in the defences. Positions which beat off the initial attacks could not hold out for ever once they had been cut off and could be dealt with at leisure by the supporting troops. The difference between the two doctrines can be likened to a wave on the seashore with the tide coming in. The German wave behaved naturally when it came in contact with a sandcastle. If it could not destroy the sandcastle it bypassed it, leaving succeeding waves to wear it down. The British wave, on the other hand, having failed in its first attempt, caused the progress of all succeeding waves up the beach to be halted until the sandcastle was utterly destroyed.

The closing down of the 1917 campaign once again saw both sides going into conference to consider what they should do to bring the war to a successful conclusion in 1918. However, this time it was the Germans who were considering offensive operations while the Allies reverted to the defensive.

The penultimate round

On 11th November 1917 a conference was held at the army group headquarters at Mons of the Crown Prince Rupprecht. It was chaired by Ludendorff and its purpose was to consider the German strategy for 1918. Russia was virtually out of the war. (The armistice at Brest-Litovsk was to be agreed on 16th December.) Italy was sitting groggily in her corner still reeling from the blow she had received at Caporetto and unlikely, whatever resuscitation her seconds gave her, to be able to do any more than try to keep her guard up for at least the next few rounds. In the west, in spite of the massive onslaughts at Chemin des Dames and Ypres, the German line still held, but it was not nearly as strong as it had been at the beginning of the year. However, a dark cloud lay on the horizon in the shape of the United States. It would only be a matter of months before the Allies received a very substantial 'shot in the arm' in the shape of the American troops which were now starting to make their way across the Atlantic. To the war-weary German troops the thought of an inexhaustible supply of fresh reinforcements meant certain defeat. At the same time the other members of the Central Alliance, Austro-Hungary, Bulgaria and Turkey, were all wavering and almost at the end of their strength. Something decisive had therefore to be done quickly. To Ludendorff's mind: 'The condition of our allies and of our army all called for an offensive that would bring about an early decision. This was only possible on the Western Front . . . The offensive is the most effective means of making war; it alone is decisive.'

Having decided on the Western Front there remained the question of whom to attack, the British or the French. There was a strong lobby for

'The Yanks are coming'. Dazzle-painted and renamed *Leviathan*, the former German liner *Vaterland* is used as an American transport

another attack at Verdun. The immediate capture of the town, which had now become a symbol for the French, would have a considerable effect on French morale, which would make exploitation considerably easier. With the French defeated they could then attack and destroy the British. Ludendorff was sceptical of this as he felt that it would be inviting the British to attack him in Flanders. Also the French had a very considerable area of country in which to fall back through, thereby giving them time and more chance to recover. He argued therefore that it was the British who should suffer the assault. They would naturally retreat towards the Channel and north of the Somme they had comparatively little room in which to reorganise. In his summing-up of the conference he pointed out that the Germans would only have enough troops to spare for one major offensive and that they '. . . should strike at the earliest possible moment, if possible at the end of February or beginning of March, before the Americans can throw strong forces into the scale'. His third condition was that it must be the British who were beaten.

They now had to select the particular sector. In planning an offensive, their methods were very different to those of the Allied commanders, who selected distant strategic objectives first and then failed to use the right tactics to achieve them. Ludendorff emphasised that: 'Tactics had to be considered before purely strategic objectives which it is futile to pursue unless tactical success is possible. A strategic plan which ignores the tactical factor is foredoomed to failure.' They had evolved the tactics and these were laid down in a pamphlet entitled 'The Attack in Trench Warfare' and all units were ordered to take notice and study it. The Storm Troops, who led the attack, were selected from among the youngest and fittest in the existing infantry battalions and formed into special units.

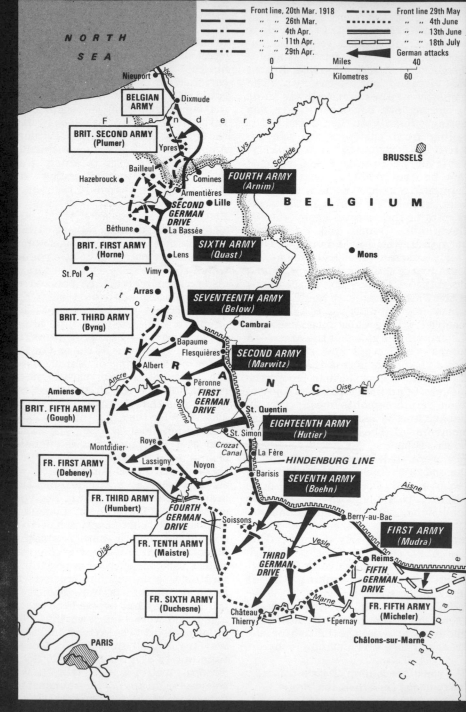

The German offensives of 1918

The 'battle units', which were to follow in their wake, were to consist of infantry, machine-gunners, trench mortars, engineers, and field artillery. Their task was to resist counter-attacks and take on strongpoints. They were to keep close behind the Storm Troops and were not to allow themselves to be held up for long, for there would always be more troops behind them who could deal with particularly stubborn positions. The whole doctrine emphasised that forward troops should take the initiative into their own hands. Instead of following the Allied principle of leaving all decisions to a formation headquarters in the rear, which could never be up to date on the complete tactical picture, junior commanders in front were encouraged to take their own decisions and act on them. For instance, if they felt that the creeping barrage was moving too slowly forward, a signalling system was arranged whereby they could contact the artillery immediately and get them to speed it up; so different to the British artillery plan, which once it had been put into effect, remained unalterable.

Bearing these tactics in mind the Germans selected a number of likely sectors from which to launch the attack. There were three main areas which seemed at first sight to be feasible. The first envisaged converging attacks to the north and south of Ypres converging on the important railway centre of Hazebrouck. These two attacks, called respectively 'George II' and 'George I', had as a disadvantage the fact that mobility would be much affected by the unreliable climate. The Germans had seen the effects of bad weather on an offensive in that area all too recently. Further south lay the Arras front, with the British sitting on the Vimy Ridge and projected attacks here and south of Arras towards Bapaume were nicknamed 'Valkyrie' and 'Mars'. Ludendorff's own suggestion was for an attack on the Somme from St

Quentin towards Amiens. It had the advantage that the Hindenburg Line could most easily mask preparations for the assault, but on the other hand his troops would be attacking over the old Somme battlefields, which again would affect mobility. Also it would mean that, in order to cut the British off from the French and then drive them into the sea, the lines of communication would become that much more stretched. It was the possibility of being able to separate the Allies that made the plan – which he dubbed 'St Michael' – so attractive to Ludendorff. Further south along the whole front other attacks were planned, particularly in the area of Verdun. It was not until the end of January that Ludendorff finally made up his mind and decided on 'Michael'.

At the beginning of November 1917 the Allies had had a conference at Rapallo at which it was decided that from now on the war would be run by a central committee, which would have representatives from each nation. As a result of political wrangling Foch, who had been Chief of Staff to the French army, found himself in the position of Generalissimo. With the closing down of the activity in the Cambrai sector it became clear that the allies on the Western Front were suffering from a dangerous state of exhaustion. The truth of the matter was that the French army, in spite of its six months convalescence, was still in a much weakened state, not so much in terms of morale as in men. The French had no more reserves of manpower to call upon and were forced to scrap three divisions completely and reduce the hundred remaining to an establishment of a mere 6,000 men each, half of the 1914 figure. Yet the British were in little better state. Lloyd George, fearful that Haig was going to embark on another Third Ypres type of offensive, purposely placed an embargo on reinforcements being sent across from England. Haig does make mention in his diary entry of 7th January 1918

127

Foch, Generalissimo of the Allied armies on the Western Front in the last year of the war

that the best way to defeat the German attack would be by continuing the attack in Flanders in order to contain their reserves. Yet entries very shortly after this make one more convinced that this was merely a thought registered on the spur of the moment and not an idea that he entertained seriously.

The net result was that Haig's sixty infantry divisions on the Western Front had each of their three brigades reduced by one battalion. Few of the battalions themselves had a trench strength of more than 500, compared with the 1914 establishment of just over 1,000 all ranks. It is important to note that this reduction only applied to British divisions and not to Colonial, which maintained four battalions to the brigade. This was one of the reasons why much of the fighting later on was to be borne by the Canadians and Australians.

It had been agreed at the Boulogne Conference of September 1917 that the British should take over more of the French line. In mid-October Haig had arranged with Pétain that the British line should be extended down to Barisis, just south of the River Oise, an extension of some twenty-five miles. Cambrai and the need to rush troops to Italy after Caporetto had caused Haig to postpone any moves to extend southwards. In December Clemenceau, the new French Premier, and Pétain attempted to force Haig to relieve the French along a further thirty-seven miles of front to Berry-au-Bac on the Aisne. This was out of the question as far as Haig was concerned, although he did agree to complete the Baresis extension by the end of January, which he did. Later, the Supreme War Council demanded a fourteen mile extension south of Baresis, but although Haig finally acquiesced under protest, the Anglo-French junction point was still at Baresis when the German onslaught came.

The main reason behind these extensions lay in the wish of the Supreme War Council for a strong central reserve to be formed behind the whole front, which could go to the aid of either the British or French if any part of their line was attacked. Although Lloyd George was much in favour of this idea, according to some, because of his desire to curtail Haig's powers by taking away some of the forces under his command, Haig was unable to spare the troops to extend his line and contribute to the central reserve. As it was, by the time he had finished re-deploying his troops he was left with a mere eight divisions for his own reserve. Foch had envisaged the French providing some thirteen or fourteen divisions to this and the British nine or ten. Even Pétain would not provide more than eight divisions, of which four were 'green' American formations, newly arrived in France. Pershing, the American commander, was not keen to see his troops split up into small packets and placed under British or French command, although he was prepared temporarily to attach bat-

Above: Clemenceau (right), the new French Prime Minister, talking to General Hunter-Weston, commander of British VIII Army Corps. *Below:* The first American troops arrive at St Nazaire, June 1917

The King of the Belgians with General Gough, commander of British Fifth Army

talions to both merely to get them acclimatized to trench warfare. He was content to wait until his army had built up enough strength to take the field as a separate entity. In doing so he was religiously following the instructions laid down by Newton D Baker, the American Secretary of War, which emphasised that '. . . the forces of the United States are a separate and distinct component of the combined forces, the identity of which must be preserved.'

Although the French felt that the attack might fall on Verdun or the Châlons sector, it was the British Intelligence Branch which accurately forecast the time and place. Charteris, the Intelligence chief, had predicted as early as 20th December that '. . . the enemy's big blow would not fall until March.' At the beginning of January Haig felt that the Germans

were capable of attacking both the British and French and was much concerned that if the attack fell on the French the British line would be seriously weakened on account of having to send reserves to help. By the beginning of March it was clear that the Germans were going to attack the British between Arras and St Quentin.

At the beginning of February the Allies were fully deployed to meet the German thrust. In the north the Belgians, under their king, held eighteen miles with thirteen divisions. Then came Plumer's Second British Army, which still held the Ypres salient with twelve divisions. From Armentières to just north of Arras Horne's First Army covered the next thirty-three miles with fourteen divisions, including two Portuguese of doubtful quality and four Canadian. Byng's Third Army held from Arras down to south of Flesquières, a distance of twenty-eight miles, with fourteen divisions. The vital sector down to the junction with the French was the weakest and Gough's Fifth Army found itself holding no less than forty-two miles with only twelve infantry and three cavalry divisions. Admittedly some ten miles of this was partially protected by the Oise as it ran through the marshy valley south of La Fère. However Gough's main problem was that the frontage which he had taken over from the French was in a very bad state of repair and he had barely two months in which to prepare it. The French were deployed with three armies, the Sixth, Fifth and Fourth, covering from Baresis to Verdun, a matter of seventy miles. The Second Army held Verdun with the First below it in the St Mihiel Salient. The southerly two armies, the Eighth and Seventh, covered thirty and seventy miles respectively down to the Swiss border. The four American divisions were located some sixty miles to the south of the St Mihiel salient, but still very much under training.

As regards methods of defence it was soon apparent that there was a vast difference in ideas between the British and French. Of the ninety-nine French divisions deployed Pétain had no less than thirty-nine held in reserve. Nineteen of these were deployed to cover any German attack from Verdun to the Vosges, while a further eighteen were 'in the Champagne barring the way to Paris. Only four of these were in any position to be able to support Gough and the final two were right up in the north behind the Belgian army. Haig had only his eight divisions and these were mainly concentrated behind Arras in the centre of his line. Thus Gough had little to call upon in the event of emergency. It seems strange that the Allies should have been so insensitive to their vulnerability at the point where their armies met. The fault for this must be laid at the door of the Supreme War Council at Versailles. With the failure of their plan for a central reserve they had fallen back on the idea of treating the French and British armies as entirely separate entities and allowed them both to go their own ways with insufficient thought as to mutual co-operation.

In the field of tactics Haig and Pétain had entirely different ideas. Pétain's study of German defensive methods, which had brought about the directives of late 1917, had convinced him of the necessity of a fluid defence. To this end he had written that: 'Static warfare and open warfare must no longer be placed in opposition. One fights in positions and between positions. These positions being more or less organised, more or less demolished, more or less quickly taken by attacks and counterattacks and, eventually, one fights outside the fortified zone, on ground free of all defended localities. At all times and on all kinds of ground in this battle, movement is one of the essential characteristics of offensive manoeuvre as well as defensive manoeuvre.' Consequently the French defence system of 1918 consisted of a very thinly held outpost line with a main position out of range of the preliminary bombardment with a reserve line behind it. By placing such a large proportion of troops in reserve Pétain retained his freedom of manoeuvre. At the same time he accepted that ground would have to be given up, but this was no bad thing as it provided a greater chance of catching an enemy attack off balance, the ideal moment for counterattacking.

The British, on the other hand, although they too had studied the German doctrine of defence at Third Ypres, came up with the wrong conclusions. The cause of the trouble lay in the fact that they had studied the wrong pamphlet, which concerned the construction of field defences as opposed to the one which concerned itself in the tactical doctrine of defence (*Die Führung der Abwehrschlact* of December 1916). As Corelli Barnett says: 'They adopted the basic German ideas of a dense net of

Cavalry move up in the vain hope of
exploiting success during the German
offensive of March 1918

machine-gun posts and fluid, mobile
grouping for counterattack, but they
tried to fit these things into the stiff
British organisational hierarchy, the
static British way of defending ground
by staying put on it. Moreover they
continued to think of machine-guns
as supporting a defence based on the
infantry, whereas the Germans
treated riflemen as escorts for the
machine-guns, the true spine of
resistance.' As a result the British
GHQ Instruction of 14th December
1917 ordered that the existing defence
system be organised into three lines.
The Forward Zone was to consist of
heavily wired-in strongpoints, whose
garrisons were to be strong enough to
force the Germans to deploy a large
number of troops to capture them.
This might have been satisfactory
against the primitive form of trench
attack with its emphasis on slow and

ordered progress, but not against the
infiltration methods of Ludendorff's
army. It merely condemned the
defenders to certain death and capture
and did nothing to slow down the
advance. The British main line, called
the Battle Zone, was two to three miles
behind the Forward Zone, which made
it, unlike the French main line,
within German artillery range. Finally a further four to eight miles
behind lay the Rear Zone, with about
a third of the defenders manning it as
opposed to the two-thirds which
German doctrine dictated. The
tragedy was that by the time the
attack came, on 21st March, only the
Forward Zone was anything like
complete. In both the Third and Fifth
Army sectors the Battle Zone lacked
dug-outs and the Rear Zone had not
been dug, unknown to the forward
troops. In the case of the Fifth Army
it was simply a line of turned turf with
not a strand of wire and was cynically
called the 'Green Line'.

As the days drew on the Germans

General von Hutier, commander of German Eighteenth Army. The tactics which he and his artillery expert Colonel Bruchmüller had used at Riga on the Eastern Front were to prove astoundingly successful in early 1918 in the West

had transferred more and more divisions from the Eastern Front, until by the beginning of February they had no less than 194 divisions in the West. Some fifty extra divisions had been brought in and the most salient features of preparations were the high quality of the staff work and the utter secrecy which surrounded the whole operation. In the front line the Germans stepped up raiding and during the period 8th December to 21st March they carried out no less than 225 raids on the British front alone, which enabled them to obtain a clear picture of the British forward defences and dispositions. The British tempo of raiding was reduced, except in the Fifth Army sector, where Gough, concerned over the state of his defences, was naturally sensitive about the progress of preparations on the other side of No Man's Land. Some British Divisions even went so far as to introduce a monthly cup for the unit carrying out the most successful raids. Elsewhere along the British

Front there was a greater emphasis on air reconnaissance, especially in view of British air supremacy.

Gough had every reason to be worried. He had no less than thirty-three assault divisions pitted against him, belonging to von Hutier's Eighteenth Army and von der Marwitz's Second Army. The larger part of this force belonged to von Hutier, who, along with his artillery expert Colonel Bruchmüller, had planned and executed the breakthrough at Riga. Byng's problem was nowhere near as difficult for he faced only the fourteen divisions of von Below's Seventeenth Army. Small wonder then that Gough made earnest representations to Haig for more divisions to be transferred to him. Haig relented finally and a week before the attack moved three divisions from his small reserve down to support the Fifth Army. However these were kept well back and remained under the control of GHQ, in spite of Gough's entreaties. By now it was known that the German attack was coming in on the 20th or 21st. On the night of 20th March a raid in the area of St Quentin by troops of the XVIII Corps captured thirteen prisoners. These belonged not to the *Landsturm* (German second line territorial) formation, which had been holding the line previously, but to a first line division. On interrogation they confirmed that the attack would start at 0445 hours next morning. There was time enough to warn all units.

At 0300 hours on the 21st the British artillery opened up with a mixture, of HE and gas shells on the German back areas, hoping to catch the German reserves as they moved up. This produced little reaction from the Germans until at 0443 hours six thousand guns opened up with a crashing bombardment. Bruchmüller's master plan allowed for the first two hours of fire to be concentrated on counter-battery work, command posts and other targets in the rear area. Again the principle of fire by survey, as opposed to pre-registration, was used. Then, apart from the heavy artillery, the Battle Zone was taken on. Finally there came the systematic demolition of the Forward Zone with a concentration of gas shells being put down on its rear, until at 0935 hours there was a five minute crescendo on the Forward Zone. Preceded by a creeping barrage the storm troops then went in. As at Riga and Caporetto their ally fog was present and the concussed British did not see their opponents until they were almost upon them. The bombardment had led to the almost complete breakdown of communications and within minutes all contact with the units in the Forward Zone was lost. By midday the Germans were through the Forward Zone almost everywhere along the front and were coming up against the Battle Zone. By now the fog was lifting, giving the defenders a better chance of seeing the attackers

German infantry advance through gas filled woods

in time to bring effective fire to bear. However in the South about the low-lying environs of the Oise the fog persisted until mid-afternoon enabling the Germans to get deep into the Battle Zone. By the time dusk fell they were through and established along the line of the Crozat Canal as far west as St Simon. Elsewhere, although deep penetrations had been made in the Battle Zone, the Germans had not been able to break out into the open country to the rear. In spite of the British preoccupation with positional defence, which had led to the sacrifice of virtually a third of the troops involved (those in the Forward Zone) there had been more of a tendency not to make useless sacrifices in the Battle Zone and a greater willingness by commanders to allow troops to withdraw to more favourable ground.

Notwithstanding the inability of the Supreme War Council to organise their central reserve, Haig and Pétain had come to an arrangement, before the battle started, that General Humbert with six French divisions would be made available to the British Fifth Army the fourth day after their assistance had been called for. Yet on the evening of the 21st Haig still remained optimistic and the wretched Gough found it impossible to convince GHQ of the gravity of the situation. Thus no demand was made on the French this day.

The dawn of the 22nd brought more fog and once more the *strosstruppen* pushed on relentlessly, closely followed up by the 'battle units'. In accordance with Ludendorff's orders to establish the right flank of the attack securely along the line of the Somme, St Simon and Péronne prior to wheeling northwards in a direction of a line Arras – Albert, the pressure came off the battered divisions along the Crozat Canal in the south. In the north, however, the fog also acted as an ally to the British, for the German artillery could no longer rely on prediction and required

good observation for its fire to be effective. As a result the Third Army was able to hold the rear of the Battle Zone in many places, although the Germans did make progress along the Cambrai-Bapaume road. It was the Fifth Army, particularly in the centre, which really suffered. For a start the Battle Zone proved indefensible because of the lack of defences, and the inability of formation headquarters to control the units under them, because of bad communications, meant that it was left to battalions, companies and even platoons to cope as best they could. They fell back towards the Green Line, fully believing that once they arrived there the defence systems would give them time to reorganise and hold the enemy off. Herbert Read, the poet, who was a major in the Green Howards, describes what happened when they reached the Green Line: 'Then I reached the line. I stood petrified, enormously aghast. The trench had not been dug, and no reinforcements occupied it. It was as we had passed it on the morning of the 21st, the sods dug off the surface, leaving an immaculately patterned mock trench.' That evening Gough sought Haig's permission to fall back to the line of the Somme and hold the Péronne bridgehead. This was given and Haig also asked Pétain to help out with the defence of this line, along with the Crozat Canal.

On the 23rd the seriousness of the situation became fully apparent to Haig and he asked Pétain to concentrate a force of twenty divisions in the area of Amiens. Pétain was reluctant because the French were expecting an attack in the Champagne, where the Germans had been carrying out artillery demonstrations as elsewhere along the front. Haig had realised that the main danger lay in the attack splitting the Allies and driving the British into the sea and was relieved when Pétain assured him that he would do all he could to keep the two armies in contact. On this day Haig had visited Gough in person at

his headquarters and '. . . was surprised to learn that his troops are now behind the Somme and the R Tortville.' He could not understand why Gough's troops had retreated so far without making some sort of stand. In fact eight of the Fifth Army divisions were little more than remnants and the Germans were faced with a yawning gap of some forty miles. As it was the French reinforcements who had been rushed up from the south to bolster the defences found themselves caught up in the headlong retreat of the Fifth Army.

Yet things were not going as well as they might with Ludendorff. Although von Hutier had achieved his part of the plan, Marwitz and Below were still finding the opposition in front of them tough and resolute and there were little signs of cracks appearing. On the morning of the 23rd Ludendorff issued fresh orders. The Seventeenth Army was ordered to turn north-west towards St Pol, Second Army was to continue westwards towards Amiens and the Eighteenth Army was to turn south-west in order to push the French away from the British. It was this plan which more than any other factor, brought about the eventual breakdown of the German attack. For, by ordering the three armies to attack in divergent directions, he was merely dissipating his strength and ignoring the cardinal rule of his doctrine of attack in failing to reinforce success, in this case that achieved by von Hutier. At the same time the strain was beginning to tell on the attacking troops themselves. The German practice of merely reinforcing forward units with men, as opposed to rotating the units, aggravated the fatigue. They were now passing over the old Somme battlefields – which slowed down mobility – and the sight of well-stocked dumps and canteens, abandoned by the retreating enemy,

A German stormtrooper poses for the camera. His main weapon was the stick grenade

Ludendorff

made them realise that the submarine campaign had not been as successful as they had been told. There was a greater temptation to be diverted by booty.

During the next few days the offensive continued with von Hutier again making by far the most progress, but the rate of advance was getting slower each day. This gave the Allies their breathing space. In the north the gallant Plumer offered up no less than twelve of his fourteen divisions in return for shattered Fifth and Third Army divisions. Pétain was now bringing up no less than twenty-four divisions from the south. More importantly, it was realised that an effective commander-in-chief was needed, to control and coordinate the Allied effort, and the Doullens Conference of the 26th officially nominated Foch for this task, giving him proper executive powers. It became apparent that Amiens was the key to success and failure on both sides and ever increasing German exhaustion gave more and more time for the Allies to bring up fresh troops.

On 28th March Rudolf Binding, a German staff officer, recorded: 'Today

The German attacks grind to a halt as the casualties mount and exhaustion sets in

the advance of our infantry suddenly stopped near Albert. Nobody could understand why. Our airmen had reported no enemy between Albert and Amiens . . . Our way seemed entirely clear. I jumped into a car with orders to find out what was causing the stoppage in front. As soon as I got near the town I began to see curious sights. Strange figures, which looked very little like soldiers and certainly showed no signs of advancing, were making their way back out of the town. There were men driving cows before them on a line; others who carried a hen under one arm and a box of notepaper under the other . . . Men dressed up in comic disguise. Men with top hats on their heads. Men staggering. Men who could hardly walk.' Exhaustion and temptation had finally proved too much and the Allies were saved. The Germans were to continue their attempts on this

front until 4th April, but their attacks were halfhearted and not pressed with the *élan* of a fortnight earlier. 28th March marked the end of the Michael offensive for on that day Ludendorff gave orders for the Georgette attack to be put into effect some eight to ten days later on the Lys. The Michael plan has often been compared to the German *Sichelschnitt* of May 1940. The Germans in 1940 succeeded for the very reasons that caused them to fail in March 1918. The aim was the same in both cases, but concentration on a single objective, the coast at Abbeville, reinforcement of success, air supremacy, the freshness of the troops (it being the start of the war in the west) and a sound administrative plan, besides low morale on the part of the defenders, gave them victory in 1940. The converse of these factors led to failure in 1918.

Georgette was what had originally been designated George, but on a much reduced scale. It will be remembered that the original plan for St George had envisaged two thrusts either side of the Ypres salient. It became apparent at the end of March that there were only eleven fresh divisions available for the attack. Hence George 2, the northern effort, was cancelled and George 1 had to be reduced from a thirty to a twelve mile frontage, between La Bassée and Armentières. Twenty-six divisions were available, but whereas Michael had its forty-seven assault divisions, here only twelve of these were of this category. The indefatigable Bruchmüller was transferred to this front to handle the artillery planning, along with much of the artillery used in Michael. Ludendorff had, however, unerringly chosen exactly the right place for another assault on the British. The Armentières-La Bassée sector was held by six divisions, of which four were in the front line. Four of these divisions were still recovering from the Michael attacks and another, which was the 2nd Portuguese Division, was in such a low state that it was about to be relieved. Only one division, the 55th West Lancashire Territorial, was fit and reasonably up to strength. Half the frontage involved was held by the Portuguese.

On the 7th and 8th of April the Germans saturated Armentières to the north and Lens to the south of the threatened area with mustard gas. At 0300 hours on the 9th Bruchmüller's preparatory bombardment opened and five hours later nine German divisions went into the attack, once again grateful for the presence of their seemingly constant ally, fog. The Portuguese broke immediately and, to use Haig's words, '. . . retired or to be more exact "ran away" through the British taking their guns with them'. Haig appealed to Foch to take over some of the British line so that British divisions could be transferred to meet this new threat, but Foch believed that the next German blow would fall on a line Arras-Amiens and would only

sanction the deployment of Maistre's Tenth Army, with its four infantry divisions and a cavalry corps, behind Amiens. He would, however, arrange for them to be moved north if the need really arose. By the evening of the 9th the Germans had broken into an area six miles deep and ten miles wide, having got through the Rear Zone. Only 55th Division in the south opposite La Bassée had held.

Next day the Germans enlarged the gap northwards up as far as the Ypres-Comines Canal, but progress was much slower, in spite of the mist. Only on the original front did progress continue to be made and Ludendorff again committed the cardinal error of failing to reinforce success. By the 19th the frontage had increased to thirty miles taking in the whole of the original George 1 to the north of Ypres, and although the advance had got to within five miles of Hazebrouck, it was now, once again nothing more than a slow push forward in the traditional manner. Once again there was time for the French to come up from the south in order to help stabilise the line. Also the defenders had learned much from the Michael attacks. Defence became more flexible and they started to employ the German methods of leaving behind booby traps and delayed action mines. Above all the Germans were not attacking with the same spirit as they had in March. Ludendorff himself wrote: 'Our troops had fought well; but the fact that certain divisions had obviously failed to show any inclination to attack in the plain of the Lys gave food for thought . . . the way in which the troops stopped round captured food supplies, while individuals stayed behind to search houses and farms for food, was a serious matter. This impaired our chances of success and showed poor discipline. But equally serious that both our young company commanders and our senior officers did not feel strong enough to take disciplinary action, and exercise enough authority to enable them to

German reserves pass through recently captured French trenches

lead their men forward without delay.' By the 30th Georgette had joined Michael in the wastepaper basket of failure.

The Germans had now lost some 350,000 men and inflicted an equal number of casualties, mostly on the British. At the same time 180,000 Americans had arrived in France. Pershing, despite his earlier determination to stand apart until the Americans were strong enough to take to the field in their own right, had already, at the end of March, put three American divisions (equivalent to six French or British) into the line under French command thus relieving French troops to support the British. To Ludendorff it appeared that the British were exhausted. The French were now propping up their ally and if he could attack the French it would cause them to remove that prop, enabling him then to deal piecemeal

with the British. Yet this had not taken into account the growing American strength and he was falling into exactly the same trap as the Allies had in previous years. He now ordered yet another offensive, this time over the well fought over battlefield of Chemin des Dames. It would take a month to prepare for this attack, a month which gave the Allies valuable time to reorganise themselves.

As early as 3rd April Foch, in his capacity as Generalissimo, had issued a directive in which he made the faulty appreciation that the Germans would make a renewed effort north of the Somme. To this end he ordered a double counteroffensive , by the French from Montdidier towards Roye to the north-east and by the British north of the Somme, between the Luce and the Ancre. This plan had been scotched temporarily by Georgette, but by the beginning of May Foch was still determined to go ahead with it. But he realised he had to build up his resources before he could attempt this. It seemed to him that, as the French and more especially the British were exhausted, the answer was to use the Americans to bolster up each of them. Pershing, in spite of his assistance in the emergencies of March and April, obstinately refused to sanction this. To his mind it was only a question of time before the main burden of the fighting passed to the Americans and he was determined that they would remain fresh until that time. So Foch had to modify his plan and directed that the Montdidier attack should become a joint Anglo-French venture. Haig, at the same time, was requested to plan an attack in the Ypres area to relieve German pressure on the vital industrial area around Béthunes. It was appreciated that the German attacks were not over. But, both the British and the French were convinced that it was the British who were to suffer yet again. Only the Americans deduced correctly that Chemin des Dames was the target, but their advice was so ignored, probably out of pique more than anything else, that four British divisions which had borne the brunt of Michael and Georgette were sent down to Chemin des Dames to 'rest'.

On 27th May the Germans struck, again using the Bruchmüller bombardment technique. They employed forty-one divisions on a thirty mile front and no less than 3,719 guns participated in the opening bombardment, which according to the defenders was the most punishing of the war. Facing them were four French divisions and three tired British ones of Duchesne's Sixth French Army. The disaster that followed was attributable to Foch's concept of defence, which was utterly different to Pétain's ideas of the fluid defence. On 5th May Foch had issued a directive to Pétain and the army group commanders,

After a French counterattack, German dead lie in their hastily-dug trench, now their grave

which laid down that '. . . it was necessary before all to dispute ground with the enemy step by step . . . there can be no question of lines of advanced posts or of observation, and of lines of resistance . . . Any retreat, even very slight, would thus play the enemy's game.' This was a direct contradiction of the Pétain concept and boiled down to the traditional 1915 type of defence of packing all one's troops in the front line. The British commanders were aghast at this, especially in the light of their recent experiences, but their remonstrances fell on deaf ears. Unfortunately Duchesne was a Foch man, having been his chief of staff at the beginning of the war, rather than a supporter of Pétain. The army group commander, Franchet d'Esperey, was of the same mould and consequently the wretched Sixth Army was packed into a strip only five miles deep with the River Aisne at their backs and a tributary of the Aisne, the Vesle, just behind this.

The result was that the forward troops, which contained the major part of Duchesne's army, after being utterly shaken by the bombardment, were decimated where they stood. One British division, the 8th, was reduced to a ration strength of 1,500 men only by the end of the day, by which time the Germans were across the Aisne. The morning of the next day took them across the Vesle. An advance of no less than twelve miles was made on that first day and this remained a record for the Western Front. Even Ludendorff was surprised: 'At the outset we were bound to anticipate that our attack would come to a halt on the Aisne-Vesle line and would be unable to get beyond that sector. We were therefore not a little surprised when we received a report about midday . . . that smoke from German shrapnel could already be seen on the southern bank of the Aisne and that our infantry would cross the same day.' In the beginning the attack had not been intended to be decisive, merely an attempt to draw away French reserves from behind the British, but the temptation to turn it into a major attack became too great and Ludendorff threw everything he had into it. By the 29th the Germans had penetrated thirty miles, to the outskirts of Château-Thierry, and less than sixty miles from Paris. However it was only a narrow salient and Reims on the Allied right held out.

Pétain did not panic and, instead of throwing the available reserves piecemeal into the fight, held them back on a line running through the eastern fringes of the forest of Villers-Cotterets, the Marne and on up to Reims. Meanwhile the German restraints were cracking and once again, as in front of Albert, temptation got the better of them and they fell off the line of march to pillage. When they came up against Pétain's defences on the next day they had lost their dash and the offensive came to an end. Taking part in this final defence were two American divisions – the first time they had faced up to a German attack, and they acquitted themselves admirably. In order to widen the narrow salient which he was in, Ludendorff was forced to carry out another attack between Montdidier and Noyon to the west. Once again Pétain was somewhat foiled in his attempt to try out his methods of defence. Foch had issued another order on 2nd June, saying that in order to prevent the German advance on Paris '. . . a foot-by-foot defence of the ground in this direction was required, pursued with the utmost energy'. General Humbert, who was defending the Noyon-Montdidier sector, was a conservative by nature and attempted to hold his front line to the last, instead of using it as a brake to slow down the German advance so that it could be dealt with by the support line. As a result von Hutier with thirteen divisions broke through the first line and occupied a seven mile stretch of the second by 1100 hours on the first day, 9th June. Pétain had, however, once again

A ravaged village in the Noyon-Montdidier area

wisely held back his reserves and he sent these in on the 11th, under Mangin of Verdun fame, and they caught the Germans, who were being held by local reserves, just as they had got across the River Matz. Ludendorff had failed in yet another attempt, but what was important about this failure was that it was not caused by virtue of German exhaustion, but because they had fallen victim to a successful counterattack.

Whatever Ludendorff did he seemed to be getting no nearer his goal of a decisive victory over the British. By now the German army was beginning to feel the effect of the casualties of the last few months, which had caused the average battalion strength to fall from 807 men in February to 692 in May. Ludendorff himself admitted that '. . . not only had our March superiority in the number of divisions been cancelled, but even the difference in gross numbers was now to our disadvantage, for an American division consists of twelve strong battalions'. The very thing that the Germans had been doing their best to prevent was now happening and the Battle of Noyon had also shown the Allies that it might soon be possible for them to resume the offensive.

Decision at last

On the 24th May Colonel Fuller, at the British Tank Corps Headquarters, produced a paper envisaging a new form of attack, which he claimed would bring about complete victory over the Germans. He produced a completely new thesis: that the enemy's command should be disorganised first and then his front would be attacked. As he said: 'Tactical success in war is generally gained by pitting an organised force against a disorganised one.' The best way to disorganise a force was to disorganise its command structure. In order to do this he laid down that the initial attack should consist of light tanks and aircraft. Assuming that the average German army headquarters was some twenty miles behind the front line, the light tanks would make directly for these, which they would reach and destroy in about two hours. Meanwhile the aircraft would bomb supply and road centres. Although the headquarters were to be attacked Fuller stressed that the signal communications

should not be destroyed for the reason that '. . . the confusion resulting from the dual attack carried out by the Medium D tanks and aeroplanes should be circulated by the enemy. Bad news confuses, confusion stimulates panic.' After the successful completion of this first phase the 'Breaking Force', consisting of heavy tanks, infantry and artillery, would penetrate the enemy's front. This would be followed by a 'Pursuing Force' of light tanks, lorry-borne infantry and cavalry, who would chase the now disorganised enemy back for one hundred and fifty miles, by which time Fuller reckoned that they would have been utterly beaten. The total requirement would be almost 5,000 tanks, which would mean a radical expansion of the Tank Corps. This the British High Command were not prepared to do at a time when infantry strengths were still low, but they agreed with the plan in principle. 'Plan 1919' was even more revolutionary than anything that had been produced up until then

Above: British Avro 504A bomber/reconnaissance aircraft, one of the tools of 'Plan 1919'. *Below:* Americans move up to Belleau Wood, the first major American engagement of the First World War.

by either side and was to become the basis of Allied methods in the offensives that lay ahead.

The Americans had tried their hand at attacking entrenchments during the last phase of the Chemin des Dames offensive. The 4th Marine Brigade attacked Belleau Wood, a German strongpoint to the northwest of Château-Thierry dominating the American lines, on 6th June. They had attempted a surprise bombardment in the German style, but failed to survey the targets beforehand and achieved little, most of the shells falling well beyond the wood. They then advanced in the traditional formation of extended line. The result was a foregone conclusion and very few reached their objectives. The problem was that in general the American High Command was not prepared to seek advice from the French and British and continued to feel that the rifle combined with American ardour was enough to overcome any opposition, however well entrenched. Belleau Wood did not fall until 25th June and only after repeated bombardments, which got heavier and heavier as successive attacks failed. By the end of the battle the Americans had acclimatised themselves to creeping barrages, light machine-guns, trench mortars and grenades, none of which they had possessed at the beginning of the battle. The battle is important for showing that the Americans started with exactly the same ideas as the Allies had in early 1915, yet, with assistance of advice learned as much in those nineteen days as the French and British had learned in three years. The spirit in which the Marines attacked had not been seen since the opening of the Battle of the Somme.

Ludendorff was planning one more assault. The spirit of the German army was on the wane. It was weakened by casualties and sickness caused by an influenza epidemic which hit the Allies as well, but not to such an extent on account of their better rations, and as the state of morale fell

Ludendorff's subordinates felt that the time for attack had now passed. But Ludendorff himself was determined to have one more attempt. He argued that: 'The battalion strength had been reduced, but was still high enough to allow us to strike one more blow that should make the enemy ready for peace. There was no other way.' He was still bent on delivering the decisive blow in Flanders, but still had to contain the French first. He therefore decided to attack the weakened French front on either side of Reims: 'Immediately following this operation we meant to concentrate artillery, trench mortars and air squadrons on the Flanders front, and possibly attack a fortnight later.' The date fixed for the attack was 15th July and for the fourth time in four months the German assault machine went into action.

Lack of secrecy in the German preparations – surprising in view of the care they had taken over their previous offensives – combined with a new French policy, which encouraged raiding operations, meant that the French soon knew what was 'in the wind'. Unfortunately, Pétain's doctrine of defence was once again ignored. Although he managed to persuade Gouraud, who was commanding east of Reims, to adopt his tactics, both Berthelot and Degoutte, respectively commanding the French Fifth and Sixth armies to the south-west of the town, remained unreceptive to his ideas, being convinced that the river was a sufficient obstacle to keep the Germans at bay. Once again the defenders on this flank found themselves packed into the forward positions. At the same time Mangin, holding the line Soissons-Château-Thierry, to the immediate west of the battle area, was alerted for a counterattack, being in an ideal position to drive eastwards across the rear of the attacking Germans.

This time the Germans had no less than fifty-two divisions massed to attack on a sixty miles front. The

Above: A near miss on a German gun position. *Below left:* General Mangin, commander of French Tenth Army. *Below right:* General Berthelot, commander of French Fifth Army.

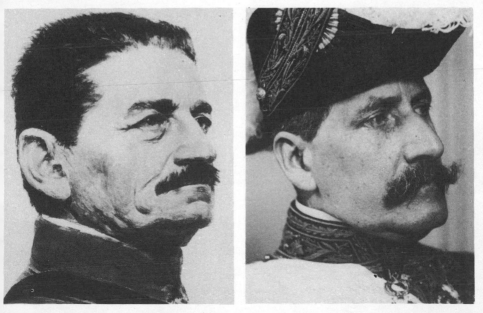

Above: Americans of the 42nd 'Rainbow' Division mop up. *Below:* A British Mark V tank in the Australian operations against the Hindenburg Line

bombardment opened up at 0110 hours on the 15th and the stormtroops went in in their accustomed manner. On Gouraud's front the French gave way, as laid down by Pétain, drawing the Germans on to their main position. Binding describes how it looked to the Germans: 'Our guns bombarded empty trenches; our gas-shells gassed empty artillery positions; only in little hidden folds of ground, sparsely distributed, lay machine-gun posts, like lice in the seams and folds of a garment, to give the attacking force a warm reception . . .' Just beyond the artillery range of their own guns they came up against the main French defences , which had been virtually untouched, and repeated attempts to storm them that night failed utterly. On the other flank the situation was very different. The defenders suffered the full weight of the German bombardment and this helped the stormtroops to bring off the brilliant feat of crossing the Marne under fire. They sliced through the French and looked almost like cutting off Reims from the south until they were brought up against Pétain's own reserves. By midday on 16th July the whole advance had come to a halt and Bruchmüller's artillery were already on their way up to Flanders to prepare for the main effort against the British.

The moment which Pétain had been waiting for had now arrived and on the 18th Mangin launched his counterattack with eighteen divisions preceded by 225 heavy and light tanks. As at Cambrai, no preparatory barrage was used and the tanks and infantry advanced behind a creeping barrage making full use of the early morning mist. The Germans were caught by surprise and by the end of the first day they had cut four miles across the German salient. The French, however, were not accustomed to exploitation tactics and the second day resulted in an advance of only two miles. In spite of throwing in de Mitry's Ninth Army, which had relieved part of Degoutte's front, and Berthelot's Fifth Army

along the Château-Thierry-Reims sector on the 20th, the chance of a breakthrough at this stage was lost. For now the German defence had tightened up and they only gave up ground because it suited them to do so. On 22nd July Ludendorff resolved to pull his troops back to the River Vesle, which ran across the base of the salient, and the first stage of this withdrawal took place on the night of the 26/27th. The Americans bore the brunt of the fighting during the latter part of the Second Battle of the Marne. Once again they suffered heavy casualties in learning the art of trench attacks, which had cost their allies so dear in years past. On the 20th, to the east of Château-Thierry they attempted to get across the Marne, while the French retook the town itself. The Germans turned tables on them by using the elastic defence technique, which meant that the preparatory bombardment had little effect and they were drawn right up to the river's edge before being subjected to a murderous fire from the defenders on the other bank. Throughout the next few days the Americans flung themselves up against the German defences and slowly inched their way forward. Finally after a particularly bloody onslaught on the 30th involving the American 4th, 28th, 32nd and 42nd ('Rainbow') divisions, which drew in all available German reserves, the Germans broke contact and withdrew behind the Vesle. The battle was over and during the last stages of it Ludendorff regretfully realised that: 'The offensive in Flanders could not bring a rapid and decisive success. According to all indications, the enemy was ready for it. If he avoided the attack, as he had done east of Reims, we should be unable to force a decision.' This is the vindication of Pétain's strategy, which had done more than anything else to bring about the final halt to the German offensives. From now on the Germans were forced to remain on the defensive, which would lead shortly to complete defeat.

Ludendorff's appreciation that the British were wearied and on their last legs was very wrong, as he was shortly to find out. As early as 17th May, before the German onslaughts on the French had taken place, Haig had instructed General Rawlinson, commander of the British Fourth Army, to '. . . begin studying in conjunction with General Debeney an attack eastwards from Villers Bretonneux.' On 12th July, two months later, Foch wrote to Haig, suggesting that, in view of the German threat in Flanders, he should mount an attack south of the Lys to forestall it. Haig demurred and instead put forward his own idea of the attack east of Amiens, which was agreed to by Foch. Foch, however, urged that this attack should take place as soon as possible, in order to make maximum benefit of the French successes on the Marne.

The dress-rehearsal for the attack about to be launched had been enacted at the beginning of July at Le Hamel. This was a small action designed at 'tidying up' the line between Villers Bretonneux and the Somme. The Germans were placed in an awkward salient, which dominated the British lines. On the early morning of the 4th, ten battalions of the 4th Australian Division, with four companies of the American 33rd Division attached, launched an attack to pinch out this unwelcome salient. There was no preliminary bombardment and sixty Mark V tanks from the 5th Tank Brigade accompanied the Australians into the attack. The utmost secrecy had been maintained and the Germans kept on edge by regularly laying down gas concentrations on their positions for every night of the previous week. As the attackers swarmed out into No Man's Land there was a brief shelling of the German positions followed by a creeping barrage. At the same time aircraft were employed overhead to bomb and machine-gun. The operation was a complete success. A penetration of one and a half miles on a three mile front cost the Allies

only 800 casualties, whilst the Germans suffered almost 1,500 captured alone, besides killed and wounded. Supply tanks were used to bring up barbed wire and pickets to assist against possible counterattacks and ammunition was supplied by parachute, for the first time in war. It had been a copybook operation and, among the Australians, particularly their commander General Monash, restored confidence in the tank, which had been so shattered at Bullecourt in April 1917.

The Battle of Amiens, launched on 8th August, was an enlarged version of Hamel. The Fourth Army was reinforced and raised to a total of thirteen infantry divisions and three cavalry divisions, along with 2,070 guns. Supported by 324 heavy tanks and 600 aircraft they were to attack along a thirteen mile front astride the Somme. To the south the French First Army under Debeney, though without tanks, was to co-operate in the attack. To support the attack no less than 120 supply tanks were allocated, along with 22 gun-carrier tanks. In order to exploit the attack two battalions of light tanks were to co-operate with the cavalry. In effect the attack had mnay similarities with phases two and three of Fuller's Plan 1919. Once again a veil of secrecy was drawn over the operation, so much so that divisional commanders did not know that an attack would take place until 31st July and the fighting troops themselves not until thirty-six hours before.

As at Hamel, the attack was launched with the infantry close up behind the tanks under a creeping barrage. As soon as the forward troops advanced the reserves were moved up behind them, following the German idea. In the centre the furthest objectives, some eight miles behind the lines, were reached by the Canadians and Australians before the day was

American troops enter the Hindenburg Line

out. Only on the wings was there disappointment. In the north the British III Corps failed to reach its final objectives because of fire from German batteries which knocked out most of the supporting tanks. In the south Debeney, who had to be content with only artillery to support him forward, achieved even less. Nevertheless there was a yawning gap some eleven miles wide in the centre, which was ripe for exploitation. Unfortunately, as at Cambrai, the Cavalry Corps Headquarters, having been given clear orders that the cavalry were to exploit forward once the final objectives had been reached, failed to give the necessary orders. Only two brigades made any attempt to get forward and the light tanks, who had been placed under command of the cavalry, learnt a lesson which they suspected to have been true beforehand. When not under fire the cavalry outstripped the tanks, but as soon as fire was opened they fell behind. As a result the tanks were tied down to supporting the cavalry instead of pushing on. Yet the odd action did prove that the third phase of Plan 1919, or indeed the first as well, was feasible. One tank, nicknamed 'Musical Box', got right in behind the German lines and shot up camps, German reserves and transport, until, after some nine or ten hours in action, it was finally put out of action by a German field gun. Then again the 17th Battalion, the Tank Corps, the only British unit equipped with armoured cars, having been towed across the trenches by the tanks, set out to cause havoc in the German rear areas, even shooting up a German advanced Corps headquarters in Framerville, and capturing documents, among them a detailed plan of the Hindenburg Line between the Oise and Bellicourt, which was to become most useful the following month.

Ludendorff wrote of the first day of the battle: 'August 8th was the black day of the German army in the history of this war.' The official German monograph on the battle supports this: 'As the sun set on the 8th August on the battlefield the greatest defeat which the German army had suffered since the beginning of the war was an accomplished fact.' Yet both the British and the French had suffered similar penetrations during the German offensives, but had not been filled with such gloom. The truth is that Amiens was very much like the victory at El Alamein in the Western Desert twenty-four years later, or the post-Gettysburg operations in the American Civil War. The irretrievable damage had already been done at Noyon and on the Marne, just as Rommel had had made his last thrust at Alam Halfa and Pickett's charge had been repulsed on the third day of Gettysburg.

This fact was to be borne out on the following days. Whereas the German attacks from March to July had maintained their momentum after the first day, the British did not. The problem was that they had to rely on mechanical means rather than human endeavour. Only 145 tanks were fit for action on the second day and at the same time the Germans were pouring in reserves. Gains of up to three miles were made, but in the words of the Official History the attack was of 'a very disjointed nature.' By now the old Somme battlefields were reached and these slowed down the attack even more than they had the German attack in March. On the third day only sixty-seven tanks were available and gains were even less. After attacks on the the 11th had produced gains of only hundreds of yards the attack was stopped. It is interesting that the proportion of tank casualties increased from day to day and the infantry casualties increased at much the same rate. General Monash was disappointed that the orders for the advance on the second day were so cautious: 'I should have welcomed an order to push on . . . in open warfare formation.' Yet without sufficient reserves of tanks this was impossible and the tiredness of the troops, unused to such rapid advances, put paid to this. In spite of the apparent success of the first day the British had still failed to comprehend the maxim of 'reinforce success' and also only forty-two heavy tanks had been allotted to the reserve. There was still too much of a tendency to believe that tank crews were 'supermen', who could go on fighting day after day, in spite of the fumes, intense heat and stress in their narrow confines. Tanks, too, required maintenance to keep them going and this could only be done after the day's fighting, thus robbing the crews of precious sleep, something one suspects that even Fuller disregarded in his Plan 1919. Perhaps the core of the problem lay in the fact that, having achieved the initial objectives, no clearcut orders were given for the ultimate goal. The Germans, as we have seen, applied the tactics which they were capable of to their plan and then worked out the objectives, but again not to the ultimate. The British had changed their methods of planning, and now did the same as the Germans, rather than consider ultimate objectives and then try and adapt tactics to achieve this. At Amiens they showed that they had not been able to develop the system of planning any further than their opponents.

All the same the Battle of Amiens acted as a signal for a general advance along the whole front. Although Foch wanted Haig to maintain his efforts on the Fourth Army front, Haig realised that this would be expensive and urged that he be allowed to make fresh attacks elsewhere along the British army front. In the meantime Debeney had captured Montdidier on the 9th and to his south the Third French Army pushed on towards Noyon and finally on the 18th Mangin also had attacked and two days later had the heights above the Aisne firmly in his hands.

While the French attacked successively southwards Haig prepared to do the same northwards. On the 22nd Byng's Third Army attacked on a front Beaucourt-sur-Ancre to Mowenneville with 200 hastily scraped together tanks. The early morning mist enabled the first objectives to be captured with ease, but later the mist cleared and the tanks suffered heavy casualties from German artillery as they moved upon the enemy's main line of resistance. This caused some disorganisation and Byng had to pause next day to sort his troops out. Haig was annoyed by this, believing that the Germans must not be given the slightest chance to recover. While most were still believing that the war would last into 1919 Haig was convinced that every effort must be made to reach a final decision before the end of the year. 'We are engaged in a "wearing out battle" and are outlasting and beating the enemy. If we allow the enemy a period of quiet, he will recover, and the "wearing out" process must be recommenced.' To this end he issued an order on the 22nd: 'It is no longer necessary to advance step by step in regular lines as in 1916–17 battles. All units must go straight for their objectives, while reserves should be pushed in where we are gaining ground.' The lesson of reinforcing success had finally been learnt.

Rawlinson had managed to capture Albert and so the British armies were now poised all along the edge of the old Somme battlefields. On the 23rd both armies moved forward once more, slowly forcing the Germans back through the tangled maze of trenches. Finally on 26th August the First Army under Horne attacked on the Arras front and advanced up against the junction of the Hindenburg Line and the Wotan Line. This operation finally forced Ludendorff to withdraw to the fastnesses of the Hindenburg Line. The fighting from the infantryman's point of view had changed radically. A young officer of the Royal Welsh Fusiliers compares it with that of the First Battle of the Somme: 'Then we attacked en masse . . . and fought for

Above: St Quentin seen from a British position in April 1917. It was not to be captured until October 1918. *Below:* September 1918. American troops advance through barbed wire. The man on the right has just been hit

yards of ground thickly held by an enemy with no thought of retreat. Now the front in movement was wide and elastic, the fighting was open, and we were attacking positions from the flank. On our immediate front were only courageous rearguards, well supported by artillery, covering their retreating main body.' The leading infantry elements now advanced in a series of short bounds in order to facilitate the use of artillery support. Artillery observation officers accompanied them, as well as trench mortars, which were found to be particularly useful in dealing with machine-gun nests. If the leading troops came up against opposition they were encouraged to engage it with fire and work their way round to a flank at the same time. This called for a much greater emphasis on musketry than had hitherto been the case and as one divisional report on the operations succinctly put it: 'Owing to the lack of training fire control and fire discipline was absent and fire to support movement rare in application.' It soon became obvious that line communication did not work in this new style of fighting and once again forward of brigade headquarters the traditional methods of visual and runners had to be used. Aircraft contact patrols were found immensely useful and the practice of resupplying ammunition by air had become commonplace. It is interesting to note that generally the leading troops suffered much more from the German artillery than machine-guns; undoubtedly the Germans were placing greater emphasis on the use of artillery as their main weapon of defence.

Besides retreating to the Hindenburg Line as far south as Soissons the Germans also surrendered most of the ground they had captured in April in their Lys offensive. It was the signal for the Allies to pass from individual efforts along the front to take to the general offensive. 'Tout le monde à la bataille!' as Foch cried, and in a directive dated 3rd September he laid down that 'the British Armies, supported by the left of the French Armies' were to 'continue to attack in the general direction Cambrai-St Quentin.' 'The centre of the French Armies' was 'to continue its actions to throw the enemy back across the Aisne and Ailette.' The American army, on the right, had as its first task the pinching out of the St Mihiel salient and then was to launch 'an offensive in the general direction of Mezières, as strong and violent as possible, covered on the east by the Meuse and supported on its left by an attack of the [French] Fourth Army.' At the same time the advance was to be extended up to the North Sea by an Anglo-Belgian attack in the Ypres area.

The Americans moved first on 12th September. In order to erase the St. Mihiel salient Pershing planned to throw in one American and two French divisions on its left, contain as many Germans as possible with three French divisions in the centre and attack with six American divisions on the right. A four hour bombardment opened at 0100 hours and then the attack went in accompanied by French Renault light tanks and the usual creeping barrage. The Germans had, in fact, commenced their withdrawal the night before and hence much of the bombardment fell on empty trenches and the attack satirically became known as 'the sector where the Americans relieved the Germans.' All the same the Americans did impress their ally, especially in their methods of getting through the German wire. 'Trained teams of pioneers and engineers, with Bangalore torpedoes, wire cutters and axes, assisted in opening gaps in the masses of barbed wire protecting the German positions. The leading troops themselves carried along rolls of chicken wire which was thrown across entanglements here and there, forming a kind of bridge for the infantry. Within twenty-four hours the salient was no more, but the Americans were then halted and experienced the frustration of watching while the Germans hastily dug themselves in on the Michel Stellung to the rear of the salient. Pershing himself felt that: 'Without doubt, an immediate continuation of the advance would have carried us well beyond the Hindenburg Line and possibly into Metz, and the temptation to press on was very great, but we would probably have become involved and delayed the greater Meuse-Argonne operation, to which we were wholly committed.' Many Americans were bitter towards Foch for stopping the Americans in this, their first independent operation, but besides Pershing's feeling that it would have interfered with the main plan it was also undoubtedly clear that the American army still had a lot to learn about the art of handling large numbers of troops and the advance might well have quickly broken down.

This inexperience was clearly brought out when the Americans, along with Gouraud's Fourth French Army, commenced their attack towards Mezières. In spite of using tanks and aircraft and a superiority of eight to one, the American First Army could only penetrate to a depth of three miles instead of the eight confidently forecast by Pershing. Admittedly the wooded, broken region of the Argonne favoured the defensive and the Germans had prepared four defensive lines to a depth of fourteen miles. Further gains were made on the second day, but things were starting to go wrong with the American machine. There was a failure to move up guns, communications broke down and supplies failed. Only the ardour of the 'green' American troops kept them going, but this was not enough and by 1st October Pershing was forced to bring a halt to the attack, thus giving the Germans time to prepare for the next blow in that sector.

The second blow in Foch's great offensive was struck by the British on 27th September. The right wing of the First Army and the Third Army's left wing, having attacked on a narrow front, fanned out and established themselves just short of the Canal du Nord. The main effort against the Hindenburg Line came two days later when the Fourth Army, after a fifty-six hours bombardment, the first eight of which consisted of gas shells, attacked on a nine mile front with the 46th British and 27th and 30th American Divisions spearheading the attack. To start with things did not go well. Owing to a misunderstanding (that some German posts were in American hands before the bombardment started), a portion of the line in front of the 27th Division was left untouched and consequently they were kept pinned down all day by the German machine-gunners. In spite of this the 30th division on their right pressed on into the German defences. At this point they should have allowed the Australians to pass through them, but instead pressed on without properly clearing the Germans from their deep dugouts. These then rose up and fired at them from behind and the Australians were consequently held up in trying to clear this menace. Only the 46th Division on the right achieved complete success. Taking advantage of the mist they got across the St Quentin Canal achieving complete surprise and the 32nd Division, accompanied by light tanks, passed through them, to reach the rear of the Hindenburg Line by the end of the day. By 5th October the Allies were fighting their way through the open country beyond. Meanwhile the Belgians and British Second Army had recaptured the Passchendaele Ridge in a single day's fighting on the 28th, but as with the Americans in the south, the supply system broke down and the attack ground to a halt. This time it was inexperience on the part of the Belgian headquarters, which had spent the whole war on the defensive up until now, which caused the breakdown. Thus only the British attacks on the Hindenburg Line were really decisive and in the centre the French were still

German prisoners taken by the Americans on the first day of the St Mihiel assault are marched to the rear

waiting for the favourable moment, when the German reserves had been all drawn to the flanks, to attack.

The end was now in sight. Bulgaria signed an armistice on 29th September, and the breaking of the Hindenburg Line came as a last straw to Ludendorff, who was already a dispirited man. On 3rd October Germany and Austria asked President Wilson for an armistice. Yet if Ludendorff was beaten his army was not and October proved to be a month of hard and bitter fighting. The Germans withdrew slowly with their rearguards constantly turning round to keep the Allies at bay and away from the main force. Attempts by the Americans to get going again in the Argonne did not come to much and it became apparent that Foch must pin his hopes on the British efforts. Throughout the month Haig pushed the Germans back towards the Ardennes. This forced the Germans to pull back in the south in order to prevent themselves from being entirely outflanked. In turn the French started advancing in the centre and the Americans made renewed efforts on the right. The German retreat became more and more rapid and the Allies found it difficult to keep in contact. When the end came on 11th November it was just as well for all the Allies were exhausted and lacked the means to undertake a rapid pursuit. What tanks there were had long since been used up and were unable to keep up with the advance. Horsed cavalry was no match for the determined German rearguards and motorised machine-guns and armoured cars were few in number.

The end came in 1918, not because a technique had been satisfactorily developed successfully to overcome an entrenched enemy, but because of the sheer exhaustion of the Germans. The effects of the Allied blockade, discontent and sickness at home, combined with the fact that the manpower barrel was virtually empty, were the main factors which brought about defeat. The Allies, on the other hand, had received a 'shot in the arm' with the arrival of the Americans, and if there had not been the determination by the Allied commanders, Haig in particular, to seek a conclusion by the end of 1918, the war would have lasted only a few months longer. The blockade and the ever increasing American presence would have seen to this.

It has been fashionable to criticise the generalship on the Western Front, an easy thing to do with hindsight. Furthermore, all commanders tend to be judged in comparison with the great generals of history, the Caesars and Napoleons. Not every war, by any means, automatically produces a great commander and it is scarcely fair to blame the generals for their failure to be 'supermen'. Some admittedly prove themselves abler than others, but it must be remembered that they were all faced with an entirely new situation, of which they had had no previous experience themselves. The task of the general in war is to win victories and these are not won by sitting still. Sooner or later one must attack and they did their best to do this with the tools available.

The tactics involved on the Western Front in 1917–18 were not to come into

The St Quentin Canal after its capture by the British 46th Division

November 1918. The trench war is over: German troops pull back across the Rhine at Bonn in accordance with the Armistice terms

their own until over twenty years later. The French and the British chose, except for a few, to forget the lessons they had learnt during the last twelve months of the war. Whereas the British believed that the four years of trench warfare were little more than a bad dream and tried to forget them, the French believed that entrenchments were to be their defence for the future. They pinned their hopes on the Maginot Line, thereby forgetting Pétain's doctrine of mobile defence which had proved so successful in 1918.

The Germans, as a result of the peace terms, had to construct a new army. The traditions of the old Imperial Army were deliberately forgotten and they made 1918 their startingpoint. Although they had used the tank little themselves they fully appreciated its capabilities. They took note of the writings of the British and French tank enthusiasts, Fuller, Hobart, de Gaulle, Liddell Hart and Martel, whose own countrymen did not. Combining the Plan 1919 concept with their own techniques of infiltration and using machines that were now mechanically reliable they produced the *Blitzkrieg*, which was to be their tool of victory in Europe during the years 1939-42.

Bibliography

The Sword-bearers by Correlli Barnet (Eyre & Spottiswoode, London)
The Private Papers of Douglas Haig 1914-19 edited by Robert Blake (Eyre & Spottiswoode, London)
The Somme by Anthony Farrar-Hockley (Batsford, London)
Memories of an unconventional Soldier by J F C Fuller (Nicholson & Watson, London)
Foch: Man of Orleans by Sir Basil Liddell Hart (Penguin, London)
The Tanks, volume 1 by Sir Basil Liddell Hart (Cassell, London. Praegar, New York)
1918: *The Last Act* by Barrie Pitt (Cassell, London)
The Western Front 1914-18 by John Terraine (Hutchinson, London)
The First World War by Richard Thoumin (Secker & Warburg, London)